KARL KERÉNYI

GODDESSES
of SUN and MOON

Translated from German by Murray Stein

Spring Publications, Inc.
Dallas, Texas

Dunquin Series 11

Translation © 1979 by Spring Publications, Inc.
Third Printing 1988

ISBN 0-88214-211-9
Library of Congress Catalog Card Number: 79-127206

Published by Spring Publications, Inc.; P.O. Box 222069;
Dallas, Texas 75222. Printed in the United States of America

International Distributors:
Spring; Postfach; 8800 Thalwil; Switzerland.
Japan Spring Sha, Inc.; 12-10, 2-Chome,
Nigawa Takamaru; Takarazuka 665, Japan.
Element Books Ltd; Longmead Shaftesbury;
Dorset SP7 8PL; England.

Acknowledgments for quotations from other works have been made in the appropriate places in the text by the translator. The titles and original place of publication of each of the four essays in this book and details of original publication of each essay can be found in the Afterword by Magda Kerényi, below.

For the second printing, Sven Doehner and Catherine Meehan provided color guidance, Patricia Mora and Maribeth Lipscomb redesigned and produced the cover. The inset derives from a photograph of "Aphrodite riding a Goose" (from a white-ground attic kylix by the Pistoxenos Painter, British Museum D 2, London), gratefully received from Professor Dr. Hans Peter Isler, Director of the Archeological Institute of the University of Zürich.

CONTENTS

I. CIRCE

The Sorceress

If we were to speak about the sons of Helios in the manner of antiquity, it would always be necessary to tell about the Sun God himself. He is himself already a "son": Hyperionides. Conversely, when his father Hyperion is named, the tale is really about him. Only the father, who bears this Titan name, was allowed to be Titanic. But in Homer Helios too has this name, just as the Goddess Athene has her other name, Pallas. And even Phaethon, who is Helios's son in post-Homeric mythology, is also his father and, like him, Titanic. His Titanic fall is well known. He mounts the sun-chariot and oversteps "the limits" of the post-Titanic order. For this reason Zeus strikes him down with the lightening bolt, and he falls into an ancient river of the sun, the Eridanus. Phaethon, "the Illuminator": this is how Helios himself is denoted in the *Iliad* and the *Odyssey,* and just as Hyperion Eelios does, so *"eelios phaethon"* testifies to the identity of father and son.

Helios is a father also by virtue of having daughters. In the *Odyssey,* two daughters of the Sun tend the cattle of Helios: Phaethusa (the feminine form of Phaethon) and Lampetie (whose name also means "the illuminator").

1

If one also takes into account the later story about Phaethon, there are actually three sisters—besides Phaethusa and Lampetie, Aigle, "the bright" or simply "light"—and more. They mourn their fallen brother, and in their grief, they are transformed into poplars, luminous trees by the side of the Sun's river out of which there flow golden tears of amber. But they still go on existing too, serving the father; they are the Heliades, who harness the horses of the Sun for the philosopher Parmenides. In these figures there appears to us that mysterious femininity, that sisterly helpfulness and goldenness of young women, which the Greeks perceived in the sun in addition to Helios' fatherhood. The feminine gender of the German *"Die Sonne"* also alludes to this. The ancient Latvians celebrated precisely this in their songs about the Sun's daughters and the Mother Sun. "Yea, great is my kinship," says the maternal Sun Goddess in one of the songs, and that kinship is primarily of the female sex.

At this point we confront a notable phenomenon in a primal orientation to the world. Beside the mythologem of the paternal power of the Sun—or, considered from the opposite viewpoint, beside the purely solar aspect of the masculine life-source—there are mythologems of sunlike women. We want to take both "sunlikeness" and "woman" with equal seriousness in this matter. We would be stepping outside of mythology, which is an intelligible language to be heard, and we would be encountering it as something alien, if we were to explain the Sun-women as merely an accidental feminine expression for the sun. What is being spoken of here has somehow to do with the sun and with woman. We know that the Moon Goddesses have at least as close a connection to women's vicissitudes and to feminine nature as they have to the moon itself. Moon and woman are equivalent elements in the story of the abducted and slain, yet always reappearing, divine maiden, in the mythologem of the Queen of the Underworld, Persephone.[1]

We are thoroughly acquainted with the lunar element in the nature of the Greek Goddesses, and the association between the lunar and the feminine is familiar. All the more puzzling, then, appear to us the daughters of the Sun, who seem to have inherited something from the nature of the father and who also seem to reveal it. Expressed in the language of mythic genealogy: the meaning of their daughterhood, the meaning of being a Heliade, would be to show the nature of Helios under a new aspect, through a specific relation. But do they not bring something of the other side with them? It is not meaningless that the mother of Phaethusa and Lampetie has a lunar name in the *Odyssey*: she is named Neaira, the "new," just like the Latin Juno, which is a feminine form of *"iuvenis,"* only that there one thinks of a young woman, here of a new moon.

Let us review what has been transmitted to us concerning the mothers who bore Sun-children, as this material has come to us through Homer and Hesiod and in connection with the tale of Phaethon. The mother of the Sun's daughters who guarded the cattle was Neaira. In the *Odyssey*, another Sun-daughter, Circe, plays a much larger role. Her mother is named Perse, a name which is related, as the primary feminine form, to the secondarily masculine Perses or Perseus (originally a solar name), exactly as Basile is related to *"basileus."* Instead of Perse, Hesiod calls her Perseis, as though she were the daughter of Perses, like Hecate, who aside from Selene herself was perhaps the most lunar of all Greek Goddesses. In Hesiod this Perseis, who is not identical however to "Perseis" Hecate, appears in the list of the daughters of Okeanos. In this list are found also a Uranie (a "heavenly one") and an Elektre, the feminine of *"elektor,"* which in Homer was a name for Helios, like "phaethon." Hesiod's Perseis corresponds exactly to the Homeric Perse, who was a daughter of Okeanos. But with the name Perse she stands before us, in her most original form. Not only the mother of Helios's children, who for Hesiod is merely a nymph and one of many Oceanids, she is also the wife of Helios, the queen to whom Helios goes in order to become more essentially himself, more father and king and perhaps also more essentially—Sun.

The poet of the *Odyssey* may wish to denote different divine women, both lovers of Helios, by the names Neaira and Perse, but the mythological situation remains the same. The Sun God finds the reception that is essentially suitable for him, that completes his paternal and royal nature. That reception must be a *Proteron* (a self-evident preliminary event) not only of all of Helios's children but also of the paternal-kingly Helios himself. Previously this is related to Hyperion, who is, as it were, a pre-Helios. The original receiver, Theia, need not however be a pre-Perse. The sun-receiver and the sun-bearer can always be the same person. The different names simply refer to different sides of her mysterious nature. And none of these as precisely suits that mysterious property of hers through which she, as Pindar expresses it, bestows golden value (which means, most likely, giving the sun its solarity) as does the basically feminine solar name, Perse.

The names which are handed down in connection with the story of Phaethon illuminate her nature from another side. Or, to put it more precisely, they throw a shadow in the place that is lit up by the purest gold. If the mother of that young Helios, the Sun-child Phaethon, is named Klymene, the "gracious," and if this name seems to us suitable for the queen of the Underworld, then the name of the husband beside her is King Merops, an equivalent to "primal man." According to another tradition she herself was Merope, the "human female," and her husband, Phaethon's father, was named Klymenos, which is more closely related to the Lord of the Dead than it is to the Sun God. It is he who, after all, *"vocatus atque non vocatus audit"**—always grants a hearing. The names Merope-Merops, Klymene-Klymenos establish the shadowy, death-dealing element in the character of the queen and spouse of the Sun. Does not the poetic intuition of Spitteler bring together the inherent queenly majesty of Hera and the granting of power—and mortality? The mortality of the queen, from whom Zeus himself received world dominion, was a remarkable thought right out of the depths, unintentionally in harmony with the Klymene and the Persephone mythologems. Certainly the word "queen" also means something purely human to us that has nothing to do with the shadow and darkness of death. As such it expresses one possibility of feminine being, perhaps one of its original forms, like "mother" or "maiden." This is certainly something that should be taken as seriously as "sunlikeness" and "woman." At this point we know only that the mythologems of the Sun-daughters presuppose as much the mysterious primal queen as they do the paternal, golden Titan. Do not the descendants tell us something more about the nature of the ancestress?

One daughter of Perse and Helios was Circe, another was Pasiphaē. We should be familiar with Circe from Homer. But do we really know her? Do we not find it surprising that, at hearing her name, the first Sun-daughter to meet us in Greek literature is the notorious, even infamous sorceress?

Let us attempt to make her acquaintance just as the sense of the *Odyssey* would allow, unburdened by prejudices which themselves have an antique origin. There the mythologem of this sunlike woman seems rather

---

*This is a version of the famous motto above the doorway of C. G. Jung's home—*Tr.*

like a fairytale. It is the tale of a Goddess "beautifully alluring, majestic and melodic," as Johann Heinrich Voss expresses her Homeric qualities in his German translation. In the Greek she is "frighteningly powerful," having a seductive and more shrill than melodic song. If this reminds us of our own fairy tales, it is only because the stories about the pre-classical dieties of the Greeks but rarely found entry into their classical literature and were brought close to the human in ways other than were common in the case of the great Olympians. Something archaic permeates the Homeric style and translates us into the mood of the timeless wilds of original mythmaking.

The wilds are there literally. The location of Aiaia, the island of Circe, is indicated in the *Odyssey* with words that place it — as we know already — beyond east and west. Let us hear this "place definition" now in the translation of Richmond Lattimore, which will be used through the rest of the text.

> Dear Friends, for we do not know where the darkness is nor
>   the sunrise,
> nor where the Sun who shines upon people rises, nor where
> he sets . . .   (Book X, 190-192)

This is the complaint of Odysseus, although he has already experienced several sunrises and sunsets on the island. There was a special reason, rooted in the mythological perception of landscape forms, why the Greeks believed they recognized the island of Circe,

> . . . where lies the house of the early Dawn, her dancing
> spaces, and where Helios, the sun, makes his uprising,
>   (Book XII, 3-4)

off the west coast of Italy, at what is today Monte Circei. This place is connected to the mainland by a swampy path — called, before their draining, the Pontic swamps; earlier it was separated from the mainland by the same swamp and was thus an island wilderness. In this place, surrounded by sea and swamp, whose headlands were still covered with forests when I visited the place, and whose landscape in the moonlight I experienced as almost enchantingly bewitched, that great archaic Goddess, whose silhouette we discover around Circe if we read the tenth book of the *Odyssey* carefully, could well be at home.

It is in itself no great surprise that Odysseus, having already spotted the smoke of the Goddess's home — the *"megara"* of Circe — "through undergrowth and forest" (X, 150), brings down an annually large stag, "a very big beast" (X, 180). This entirely natural encounter with such a stag indicates also a specific realm: the realm of the Great Goddess of the wilds. We are further reminded of the *"Potnia theron"* (the Mistress of wild animals) when the companions who have been sent ahead reach the palace of Circe:

> . . . all about it there were lions, and wolves of the mountains, whom the goddess had given evil drugs and enchanted, and these made no attack on the men, but came up thronging about them, waving their long tails and fawning, in the way that dogs go fawning about their master, when he comes home from dining out, for he always brings back something to please them; so these wolves with great strong claws and lions came fawning on my men, but they were afraid when they saw the terrible big beasts. (Book X, 212-219)

These are bewitched animals, transformed by Circe's pernicious medicine. Were they originally humans? Eurylochos later assumes this, after the

7

companions of Odysseus had been changed into pigs and transformed back again. But it is also possible, and more probable in relation to the whole story, that the transformation into pigs was specially reserved for the human visitors of Circe. Not that Homer wanted to moralize here, as even his antique expositors have done. He portrays only those forms of being which are possible in the realm of Circe, and this divine sorceress has as much to do with the chthonic world as Demeter and Persephone do, whose sacred animals are pigs. The point is that under the sign of the seductive Circe, who in this seductiveness is also hetaera-like, what happened to the companions of Odysseus can happen to people: namely, they can be transformed and disappear into a pig-existence. Those other bewitched predatory animals, however, may originally have been ordinary wild lions and wolves. What they have learned through the bewitchment signifies a great deal: they stand upright — this is the literal meaning of that fawning "leaping up"; they have been transformed into the cultic heraldic animals of the *"Potnia theron."* In the eyes of Odysseus's companions they behave like dogs, which beside a great Goddess is fitting behavior for her favorite animals.

Archaic representations of the great Mistress of animals, flanked by her wild darlings, stand behind the much more humanized Homeric portrait. We are not getting behind this work of art into a mythology which is irrelevant for the poem of Circe. For this poem facilitates, in a more humanly proportioned way, our approach to the characteristic magic of the older mythological phenomena. In the realm of the Great Goddess, magic was still an immediate divine power, not something artificial, not a sorcery. Another portrait, also in the Homeric style, shows us that the virginal Artemis is not the only genuine descendant of the pre-Olympian *"Potnia theron.*" A Homeric Hymn depicts Aphrodite as the Mistress of wild animals (translated here by Charles Boer):

> . . . Behind her moved grey wolves, fawning on her, and
> bright-eyed lions, bears, and quick, insatiable panthers.
> When she saw them she felt joy in her heart, and she put
> longing in their breasts, and immediately they all went into
> the shade of the valley in twos to sleep with each other.
> (*The Hymn to Aphrodite,* I)

The Hymn has Aphrodite appearing with the entourage on a high mountain meadow of "Ida, rich in springs' (line 68), where the Near Eastern Great Mother of the Gods and Mistress of animals, Cybele, has her home. Aphrodite must, in that place, be a manifestation of her, just as Anchises, whom Aphrodite visits and blesses, must be the humanization of Agdistis, the masculine half of the primal Goddess of many names, among them Cybele. The fate of Agdistis was the destruction of his manhood, so that the feminine element in the image of the Great Goddess could rise to supremacy. In the cult of Cybele, this Mistress of mountains and wilds, frankly promotes the sacrifice of masculinity. This is the danger which threatens all of her favorites, every Attis. But let us hear the warning of Hermes, as he furnishes Odysseus with an antidote and with advice against the magic of Circe:

> . . . she will be afraid and invite you to go to bed with her. Do
> not then resist and refuse the bed of the goddess, for so she
> will set free your companions, and care for you also; but bid
> her swear the great oath of the blessed gods, that she has no
> other evil hurt that she is devising against you, so she will not
> make you weak and unmanned, once you are naked.
> (Book X, 296-301)

9

CIRCE

Circe is, in such works, the successor to a still greater Goddess. And her sorcery, likewise, is an imitation, in that every magical act must imitate an unmediated, powerful, divine sorcery. What offers itself as such primal divine sorcery is the all-transforming power of love. In a fortunate love encounter, power and love are balanced; moreover, the one is also the other. What produces unfortunate love is that disturbance of balance which appears as love-magic, as a wish to arouse love through power, rather than the impersonal awakening of love as a power over the lovers. Every other kind of sorcery, indeed the whole of magic, stands under the sign of the simple will to power and in relation to love-magic is secondary. Following this line of thought, Aphrodite has to be the original sorceress. In Greek mythology, the original sorceresses were granddaughters of the Sun: Medea and, before her, Circe. But this latter one is like Aphrodite, whom the Hymn shows in the love-embrace of Anchises and the *Odyssey* shows on the love-couch with Ares. These are parallels to what Circe does as she actually fulfills Hermes' predictions.

The sudden conversion of the evil sorceress into the loving woman creates the greatest difficulty for the modern reader of the Circe tale in the *Odyssey*. But this passage does not deal with a woman, with a female human being, not even with an ordinary virago, but rather with a primal sorceress, and she is so constituted that as soon as the magical circle is broken an Aphroditean primal being embraces the one who was otherwise immune and invulnerable to her. The circle, that very real enclosure within which the power of sorcery creates its own special magical world, also runs around the palace of Circe and is present as well in her name. *"Kirkos,"* which corresponds phonetically to the Latin *"circus"* and underlies *"circulus"* (circle), is in Greek the word for circling birds of prey, in one instance referring also to the circling ambulation of the wolf, and in Homer denoting the hawk. *"Kirke"* is the feminine form of this word. It is a fitting name for a daughter of the Sun, since the solar movement is circling. Probably for this same reason the Egyptians recognized the sunlikeness of their solar sparrow hawk. For love-magic the Greeks used a smaller bird with the voice of a sparrow hawk, the wryneck, which they allowed to fly in circles during the performance of the magical act. This indicates also where the love-magic is supposed to draw its power from: from that circling power in which Circe also, as daughter, is rooted.

As primal sorceress, Circe need not deny her solar origin. She herself does not fly in circles like the Mistress of animals, who in her winged form most likely could. Even in Homer a God or a Goddess sometimes appears as a bird. But we need to keep firmly in mind that Circe, in all her activities, remains human. It is human when she strikes the companions of Odysseus with her powerful magical wand and shuts them up in the pig-sty:

> and they took on the look of pigs, with the heads and voices
> and bristles of pigs, but the minds within them stayed as they
> had been before. So crying they went in, and before them
> Circe threw down acorns for them to eat, and ilex and cornel
> buds, such food as pigs who sleep on the ground always feed on.
> (Book X, 239-243)

It is also human when she sings "at the great loom," even though we feel uncomfortably reminded, by the seductive singing, of the fatally bewitching voices of the Sirens. But the weaving! How much closer this brings her to being a truly human woman than is achieved by the eternal hair-combing of a Loreley!

11

CIRCE

It is another question whether this domesticity of a Goddess, the daughter of Helios and Perse, has to do *only* with the human level or at most with the characteristics of an ordinary sorceress. Circe's blood relations constitute Homer's explicit premise, and they must never be forgotten. "The blood sister (*"autokasignete"*) of the much-experienced Aietes," or as more precisely rendered in the translation of von Schröder "the blood sister of evil Aietes" — what is this supposed to mean? Judging from his role in the mythologem of the Golden Fleece, Aietes is a king of the underworld, the Hades side of his father. His name is associated with *"Aia,"* the "Earth," according to the same law of construction which connects the epithet for Apollo, Aigletes, to *"aigle,"* the "light." If the sunlikeness of the father was supposed to have been passed on further, to the pair of siblings Aietes and Circe, then the pair must have, besides its dark, underworldly part, also a bright, heavenly part, and this part is Circe. Her domesticity only *appears* to bring her down to earth. We need to take a closer look at her "great loom."

In that strangely mythological cultural field of the north where the Latvian songs to the sun and the runes of the mythological epic *Kalevala* were kept alive, spinning and weaving were the characteristic activities of the Sun Goddess's large kinship group. An old Swedish song runs:

> Lady Sun sat on a bare stone
> And spun her gilded distaff
> For three hours before the sun rose.

In the 41st rune of the *Kalevala,* the cosmic action of Väjnämöjen's shamanistic song is depicted as follows:

12

CIRCE

Lovely maiden of the moon
And lovely daughter of the sun
In their hands hold the weaving comb,
Lifting up the weaving shuttle,
Weaving on the golden fabric,
Rustling move the silver threds,
At the edge of the crimson cloud,
At the border of the wide horizon.

The horizon's border is specified as their "location." What they are weaving
there is told in an Estonian song, in which weaving is the activity of the "old
father," the "wise old man": of the Creator.

Warp was woven there at mid-day,
Woof by the early red of dawn,
Remainders in the sun's great hall
* * * * * * * * * * * * * * * * * * *
On the loom of the weaver woven,
From the treadle it was spun
* * * * * * * * * * * * * * *
Golden garment for the moon,
Shimmering veil for the youthful sun . . .

It was, therefore, appearances of light which were spun and woven in
this manner. This has nothing to do with a mythological explanation for a
particular natural phenomenon, but rather, as the Estonian song expressly
shows, it concerns the world's creation. The world is continuously being
further spun and woven. "Light," here, can no more be astronomical light
than "day" is astronomical day in the symbol of Helios. Life is lived in
this light, in the company of these light phenomena. To put it in the spirit
of Greek solar mythology, one would say that life is spun and woven — a

13

golden, argenteous, light-filled life. As a matter of fact, this bears on the work of the Moirai. Homer even names them Clothes, the Spinners, though usually only the first of them is named Clotho. The verb that belongs to this name has as its object not merely life but rather the substance of a life's destiny, such as Odysseus's return home. They are the frigid allocators of destiny, allied as daughter sometimes to Night, sometimes to Zeus and the righteous Themis. And one of them must always be the undoer of what has been spun. In Delphi only two of them were known: a birth Moira and a death Moira. The thread of the Greek Moirai appears to be spun not of sunlight and moonlight but of measure and death. Contrary to this appearance, however, and standing as evidence that the thread was of heavenly origin, we have the testimony of the Athenians who, in one inscription, celebrated Aphrodite Urania as the eldest of the Moirai.

Once again it is Aphrodite, the "heavenly," who leads us to Circe. The Aphroditean primal witch is also a weaver. Of course, she is not the only one in the *Odyssey* who performs this task; it was an assumed task of ancient women and in itself is nothing special. Penelope, however, who seems to be the purely human weaver in the *Odyssey*, is also the undoer. In this respect her weaving corresponds to the spinning of the Moirai. Her avian name ("penelops" means "duck") may also allude to her pre-Homeric rank: the duck figure on proto-Corinthian vases, which was emphasized in every way possible, most likely refers to a great Goddess who presides over the sources of life — and of death. But at this point we do not wish to expose the mysteries of Penelope. The evidence that "weaving" can be an expression for the conception of human life or of the human body is provided by the appearance of the weaver in symbolic grave drawings on

14

Roman gravestones and by the Greek word *mitos,* which depicts the male's semen as weaving threads and which is also the name of the primordial Cabirian bridegroom.

Dare we draw the bright daughters of the Sun down into the dark depths of life's beginnings, where two threads are woven together to create new beings? Above all else Circe is no maternal Goddess, although children of hers are mentioned: sons, and a daughter named Cassiphone. According to this name, she should be the "murderer of the brother" (another name for Medea, who would then be — as one could construe this variation of the mythologem — the daughter of the brother-sister pair, Aietes and Circe). Putting aside this survey and digression, however, we will stay with the Homeric image of Circe. And that is certainly not maternal. What belongs to the sorceress is more the atmosphere of motherhood than the creative substance of it. One is really forced to find this atmosphere, which she throws about herself through her singing, hetaera-like, even as it appears in the Homeric portrait. Circe is the one, moreover, who directs Odysseus to the underworld and even sends him there. We need only remember the Sirens to realize that the hetaerian theme even by itself is associated with the lethal realm of the underworld. These two factors together bind Circe more closely to the chthonic depths than motherhood alone would do . . .

In ancient Italy the close connection between death and hetaerism is especially palpable. As a primary attitude in that place, it is as free from moralization as is the metamorphosis of Odysseus's companions in Homer. In his play *Poenulus,* Plautus describes the house of a panderer: "Here you can see every sort of person, as if you had come to — the underworld." In another work, *The Bacchides,* the pedagogue refers to the doorway of two loose young women as the "gateway to the underworld," and we might almost be tempted to say that he is here quoting Dante, or at least the old Italian precursor of *"Lasciate ogni speranza voi ch'entrate":* "For no-one comes here but he who has given up all hope in ever being a decent human being." This is not a Plautusian exaggeration (fortunately Plautusian wit has been disentangled from original aphoristic expression, and this is also the case here) but rather the complementary counter-image to the view which allowed the walls of Etruscan graves to be decorated with sensual scenes. To this counter-image, too, belongs the fact that in Latin the hetaera is also described as a "she-wolf," while the Etruscan Hades as well appears on one famous tomb painting as a Wolf God. Corresponding to this attitude one has to recognize in Circe herself the "circling wolf," especially since in old Italy she produces, as the ancestress of the Latin primal Gods, a wolfish progeny.

A weaving and then again unraveling Goddess of birth and death, a Hetaera of death who dispenses pleasure and devours humans — these are possible images of a pre-Homeric, archaic Greek, and somewhat characteristic ancient Italian mythology, sisterly figures gracing the Homeric image of Circe, in order the more to strike a contrast with this darker image. Circe stays on the perimeter of the chthonic: she does not accompany Odysseus to the underworld but only sends him there. Only the companions of Odysseus does she banish to the chthonic condition of pigs and keep there as in a sort of underworld, but neither does she share this condition nor does she take on a corresponding animal form. She has to do with all of this, since she brings about the transformation, just as the Goddess of death works transformations – only those of the latter are more substantial. What Circe brings about and weaves does not affect the substance; it leaves the "minds" of those transformed untouched, and it remains on the periphery of the real, like the sorceress herself who lives near the edge of the world, one day's journey on this side of the outermost location, from Oceanus, from eternal Night, from the house of Hades.

There is clearly another sort of hetaerism distinct from the devouring wolfish kind. In contrast to the ancient Italic image, she reveals a Greek aspect of this possibility for feminine existence. This is not the only Greek aspect, but it precisely the one which we encounter in the heavenly realm of Aphrodite. It is just in her quality of being heavenly, as Urania, that Aphrodite corresponds to the great Oriental love Goddess, and it is probably the case that her hierodules, the temple hetaerae, came as an Oriental institution with her to Greece. But it is equally important that the Athenians recognized in Urania the eldest of the Moirai and that her sanctuary at Acrocorinthus, that heavenly high-soaring city fortress which had to be scaled as in a pilgrimage in order to visit her temple servants, belonged to the archaic Greek cults of Corinth. These cults are archaic, too, for the reason that Helios played a leading role in relation to Aphrodite. Next to Rhodos, Helios was the most worshipped deity at Corinth and in its colonies. The island Goddess Rhodos was, according to Pindar, a daughter of Aphrodite. According to one tradition, Aphrodite's temple on Acrocorinthus was constructed by Medea, who was a ruler in the kinship group of Helios – as in that of Circe also – and through only a granddaughter she nevertheless extends further the line of the Heliades.

CIRCE

All of this speaks for an ancient cultic community, and this is reflected also in the fact that Hesiod recognizes Phaethon as a temple watchman of Aphrodite, who had personally translated him into the heavens. Had the quality of sunlikeness been absent from the nature of Urania, this kind of community would not have been possible. The qualification for becoming a temple hetaera in a Greek sanctuary of Aphrodite consisted in only one thing: that she could bring something of that nature to expression. Pindar offers an encomium to a wealthy Corinthian who had donated one hundred of these holy female slaves, and in this he celebrates these servants in words which, significantly enough, also describe one of the Goddess's herds of cows. Apparently this is appropriate to the mythological-hieratic conception. The reverence in the poet's tone, which is exactly adapted to the specific situation of the young women on Acrocorinthus, would be difficult to repeat in translation. Yet, before returning to Circe, one thing must be retained. After Pindar describes that unusual mode of existence, he drops the line: "We have shown the true gold . . ."

If we perceive in Circe something hetaera-like, it is only in the sense of that golden Acrocorinthian existence. And we still have to get a feeling for the fact that in Circe we meet up with the essence itself and not with the serving, imitating, and representing of it. She reveals this essence when she says to Odysseus:

> Come then, put away your sword in its sheath, and let us
> two go up into my bed so that, lying together
> in the bed of love, we may then have faith and trust in each
> other. (Book X, 333-335)

18

CIRCE

Here there is no longer any talk about reconciliation but rather about faith and trust, about uttermost submission in undisguised self-surrender (this is the meaning of the simple Greek expression for trust), in which even the purely physical attains to the designation "true," in the same sense that Hölderlin names the sun "true." It is a part of Circe's hiddenness that she can also be "false," not through holding back but through allowing herself to exceed the human scale of the openly confiding Odysseus and thus to destroy him as a man. For this reason she must first swear the great oath. She does this because the circles of her magical power have been broken through and she has only herself left. And we behold the daughter of the Sun, after she has truthfully given her final advice, rise in appropriate majesty from the side of Odysseus:

> . . . she, the nymph, mantled herself in a gleaming white robe fine-woven and delightful, and around her waist she fastened a handsome belt of gold, and on her head was a wimple . . .

> (Book X, 543-545)

1. Cf. C. G. Jung and C. Kerenyi, *Essays on a Science of Mythology,* translated by R. F. C. Hull (Princeton: Princeton University Press), 1949.

II. MEDEA

The Murderess

Homer depicts the first daughter of the Sun, Circe, as an Aphroditean archaic sorceress at the earth's far edge. And, from the viewpoint of a solar mythology, that is the correct position for a Heliade. Considered mythologically, the Sun God constitutes not an astronomical center but rather the boundary of the world that is woven out of both his existence and human existence and has dark depths round about it. Most likely these depths are dark only from the viewpoint of human existence; at any rate, they exist only in the world-fabric and have nothing to do with the astronomical sun. If we ask about the deep darkness out of which Circe has appeared, the daughter of the Sun and an unknown Goddess, and if we raise questions about this Goddess and about Circe herself, such inquiries have meaning only in relation to the world's human element and have nothing to do with astronomical matters. But the human here is in fact conceived of globally, beyond anything individual, pressing right up to the borderline where Circe and Medea, and even much greater Goddesses, disclose their faces. If, that is, they do actually disclose them and not remain in the darkness of the "background" . . .

20

MEDEA

Circe's borderline situation is to be understood also in the following manner: in her background there is presumed to be an archaic Mother and Hetaera, a figure who deals life and death to mankind, and this figure has been released in the Aphroditean nature of the Sun's daughter and changed into something else, into an archaic sorceress. To us it seemed altogether conceivable that sorcery itself could proceed from the solar-Aphroditean term, which is the essential core of Circe, and indeed that the sorcery which is a direct, and not a "manufactured" effect, proceeds *only* from this source. But the sorcery of captivation was not without malice; it was a means for exercising power, not love, and it had to be broken by a greater power before the atmosphere of Circe's essential core could flow into her house. It cannot be denied that there is a conflict here. An evil sorcery surrounds Circe, which is precisely what antiquity knew as "sorcery." Where does this come from, and what is its source, the source of evil in a Heliade? How is it that evil sorceresses belong to the Sun's kindred, particularly Medea, who was counted the most evil of all?

Medea, this most ominous of the Heliades and even of all the Greek Goddesses, did not find a great epic storyteller comparable, for universal openness to the possibilities of being, to Homer, the poet of Helen, of Calypso, and of Circe, not to mention the Olympians. Yet the ancient lyric poets do regularly celebrate the divine daughter of Aietes, son of Helios. For Pindar she is not merely the "alien who is expert in sorcery"; she is a Goddess and a queen, the "Mistress of Colchia," who speaks sagely through a "deathless mouth." Ibycus and Simonides circulate the story that the immortalized Achilles receives not Helen but Medea as wife. This would seem to be unthinkable for the murderous and revengeful figure of the mythic Argonaut cycle, who either dismembers her pursuers and enemies personally or has them dismembered by others, unless these poets were familiar with the original meaning of dismemberment and knew of the always-resurrecting Sun God in the dismembered brother and of the always-reanimating figure in the death-dealing woman.

Such awareness was not out of the question in the time of the great lyricists. But even this does not really suffice to solve this most uncanny riddle of Greek mythology, the riddle of a divine Murderess. For the moment we are not even thinking of the Medea who murders children, who was believed to be a creation of Euripides, but only of the fratricide. Even the Hellenistic epic poet, Apollonius of Rhodes, who no longer treats the adventures of the Argonauts as actual historical material in the manner of Homer's treatment of the Circe adventure, but rather as literary material that needs to be reworked for the enjoyment and under-standing of a new public, even this artistic gilder of original gold does not dare remove the dark veil of murderousness from the radiant head of the maidenly daughter of the King. There are "givens" in the mythological material that break through even in the situations created by Apollonius. He has no choice but to construct his novel situations on the basis of the ancient givens, or to use them at least as building blocks.

Is it pure happenstance, or is it a building block of the most ancient cultic material, when in the description of the restless thoughts of the love-struck Medea there suddenly appears the basin in which the sun is mirrored? Like the reflection of the sun in the house basin's water, flashing here and there, and "circling," so the heart moves in the bosom of the young woman. And does it not indicate a deeper groundedness in mythology when the Moon Goddess — referred to by Apollonius as "Titenis" or "Titaness" — recognizes her own double in the Medea who searches for her beloved in the night? "Thus not only I . . ." is how the nocturnal Titaness begins her speech from the heavens, and with this there unavoidably appears the question as to whether the mythological image of Helios' granddaughter really represents a beautiful and lethal variation on the Sun's golden melody, or whether, its close connection to the Titan of the day notwithstanding, this image is in fact only a silvery melody from the mythological orbit of the Moon. The essential core of Medea, whether it be solar or lunar, is still buried in that obscurity which surrounds her even for Apollonius.

The Hellenistic poet preserves the distance between dismemberment, that barbaric kind of murder, and his heroine, and he softens her gruesomeness by depicting Medea as being only the lure for her brother, while Jason is the one who actually kills him. But then Apollonius goes on to tell about the murderous married couple visiting Circe. The homeward-bound Argonauts touch on that other Aeaea, the "Aeatic" ("Aiaie") island in the west. There they meet up with Circe, who is busy in the sea cleansing herself of the bloody dreams which had afflicted her as premonitions of their visit. Only Medea and Jason go with her, while the other heroes avoid letting themselves be seduced by the crafty caresses of Helios' daughter. Quickly these two settle down as suppliants at the hearth of Circe. Medea holds head in hands, while Jason sticks the sword, which he used to kill Apsyrtus-Phaëthon, into the ground. There they sit, gloomy, eyes downcast.

Circe had recognized Medea by her eyes and by the golden glance of all the Sun's children. Now she also recognized her situation and proposes a great ceremony of atonement for the cleansing of the pair. She is so eager to hear the language of her own race from the mouth of the young woman! The creation of this scene and the elaboration of the encounter between these two women, who are related through the Colchisian Sun tribe, is significant for Apollonius. An essential difference between them, which was recognized but not created by Apollonius, becomes apparent when Medea's bloody deed is not met with sympathy on Circe's part. She listens to the story about the Argonauts and guesses the fratricide. And despite the subsequent atonement, she directs the cleansed pair to leave her hearth and home. Nothing is said, not even in the form of prophesy, about the later infanticide. The two sorceresses of the Sun's family are divided by something absolutely essential. It is the difference between the net and the knife, between captivation and murder, even if this murder is meant only to renew and rejuvenate the slain.

In the ceremony of atonement and Medea's banishment from the palace of Circe, Apollonius circumscribes the riddle with which he is confronted. A granddaughter of the Sun from the mythological land of morning — for Apollonius it is "Titenis Aia," from the land of the Titans — comes to Greece. There she is worshipped: in Athens, where she is associated with Aigeus, the father of Theseus, the state's founder, not so openly but more often in the more secret family cult; in Corinth in the fortress, in the cultic sphere of the pure Sun God. She arrives stained by fratricide, yet clean nevertheless. This contradiction is bridged by Circe's cleansing, which still leaves Medea a murderess with whom the Sun's daughter, Circe, will have nothing to do even after the atonement. To Apollonius the brother-killer is also of course known as a child-killer. And

24

this certainly not only through Euripides. The great tragedian, who is the only poet in whom Medea finds a worthy portrayer, faced the same riddle, and he made it no easier for himself by placing the infanticide squarely at center stage.

In this respect Euripides goes counter to all the later tradition which, most likely even before Apollonius, tried to free the cultically venerated image of Medea from the burden of her murderous past. But would it have been conceivable for him to have been the first to attribute the grisly deed of infanticide to a Goddess who belonged cultically to Helios' sphere of light? This thought is in itself an abomination, and it is made no more probable by the fact that the Jason of Euripides already glimpses in the fratricide the preparation for infanticide. (The following translations are those of Rex Warner.)

> For your own brother you slew at your own hearthside,
> And then came aboard that beautiful ship, the Argo.
> And that was your beginning.
>
> *(Medea,* lines 1334-1336)

This beginning makes it hard to understand how the Athenians could have accepted one so heavily encumbered into their holy city. It would have been plainly a wicked imputation for Euripides himself to charge his heroine with new bloodguilt and then let his chorus ask:

> How then can these holy rivers
> Or this holy land love you,
> Or the city find you a home,
> You, who will kill your children,
> You, not pure with the rest?
>
> *(Medea,* 846-850)

25

And yet, what to logical and religious understanding presents a problem which, in the given conditions of a cult that was inherited from earlier times and could be present but could not be rationally created — did in fact take place. Perhaps it was precisely the large magnitude of this problem that attracted Euripides. At the end of the tragedy, with Jason searching for the murderess, sword in hand, Medea appears to him in a chariot drawn by dragons, the corpses of the children beside her:

> Why do you batter these gates and try to unbar them,
> Seeking the corpses and for me who did the deed?
> You may cease your trouble, and if you have need of me,
> Speak, if you wish. You will never touch me with your hand,
> Such a chariot has Helius, my father's father,
> Given me to defend me from my enemies.
>
> *(Medea,* 1317-1322)

She herself takes care of the children's burial:

> I will bury them myself.
> Bearing them to Hera's temple on the promontory;
> So that no enemy may evilly treat them
> By tearing up their grave. In this land of Corinth
> I shall establish a holy feast and sacrifice
> Each year for ever to atone for the blood guilt.
> And I myself go to the land of Erechtheus
> To dwell in Aegeus' house, son of Pandion.
>
> *(Medea,* 1378-1385)

For Euripides, too, these are not solutions but rather givens of the mythology and of the cult, facts whose problematical nature are expressed clearly enough in Jason's reply:

26

MEDEA

You hateful thing, you woman most utterly loathed
By the gods and me and by all the race of mankind,
You who have had the heart to raise a sword against
Your children, you, their mother, and left me childless —
You have done this, and do you still look at the sun
And at the earth, after these most fearful doings?

(*Medea*, 1323-1328)

The connundrum was depicted even more sharply in the song in which the Chorus attempted in vain to prevent the infanticide:

O Earth, and the far shining
Ray of the Sun, look down, look down upon
This poor lost woman, look, before she raises
The hand of murder against her flesh and blood.
Yours was the golden birth from which
She sprang, and now I fear divine
Blood may be shed by men.
O heavenly light, hold back her hand,
Check her . . .

(*Medea*, 1251-1259)

The bloodthirstiness of a Fury rages within Medea. How can it happen that this demon can assert itself in her, right next to the pure power of the Sun? That, for Euripides, is the question.

The answer is given in the very first words his tragic heroine speaks. Before ever appearing on stage, she calls from within

I hate you,
Children of a hateful mother. I curse you
And your father. Let the whole house crash.

(*Medea*, 111-114)

27

MEDEA

This "let the whole house crash" creates the tragedy, being the tragic expression of feminine nature that does not diminish the worth of the wrong-doer. On the contrary, she who was rejected by her husband and who suffered the violent separation regains, as if by a merciless law of nature, her power and exalted position only through sundering even more and cutting even deeper through that life which was once formed by him, her, and the children. The children, whose earlier purpose was to constitute that life and to insure its continuance, now have no further meaning for her than to serve her in regaining power and to be sacrificed for her exaltation. And since Medea possesses the desire for blood-sacrifice, this sacrifice, too, must be bloody.

In the manner of woman-to-woman she speaks of the reasons for this inflexibility:

> It was everything to me to think well of one man,
> And he, my own husband, has turned out wholly vile.
> Of all things which are living and can form a judgment
> We women are the most unfortunate creatures.
> Firstly, with an excess of wealth it is required
> For us to buy a husband and take for our bodies
> A master; for not to take one is even worse.
> And now the question is serious whether we take
> A good or a bad one; for there is no easy escape
> For a woman, nor can she say no to her marriage.
> She arrives among new modes of behavior and manners,
> And needs prophetic power, unless she has learned at home,
> How best to manage him who shares the bed with her.
> And if we work out this all well and carefully,
> And the husband lives with us and lightly bears his yoke,

Then life is enviable. If not, I'd rather die.
A man, when he is tired of the company in his home,
Goes out of the house and puts an end to his boredom
And turns to a friend or companion of his own age.
But we are forced to keep our eyes on one alone.
                    (*Medea*, 228-247)

This account may be time-bound in its specifics, but the relationship of a
woman to the man whom she has chosen in love yields the same situation
and gives it natural validity. For this reason there is such an emphasis on
Medea's being in love:

When love is in excess
It brings a man no honor
Nor any worthiness.
But if in moderation Cypris comes,
There is no other power at all so gracious.
O Goddess, never on me let loose the unerring
Shaft of your bow in the poison of desire.

Let my heart be wise,
It is the gods' best gift.
On me let mighty Cypris
Inflict no wordy wars or restless anger
To urge my passion to a different love.
But with discernment may she guide women's weddings,
Honoring most what is peaceful in the bed.
                    (*Medea*, 627-641)

Medea's triumphant words to Jason at the end of the play accord
with a domineering woman's passionate grip on marriage as something
given by nature:

MEDEA

No, it was not to be that you should scorn my love,
And pleasantly live your life through laughing at me . . .
(Medea, 1354-1355)

And so for Euripides, despite the infanticide by which she punishes her
spouse, nay even because of it, she remains "the noble granddaughter of
Helios." Or, seen in a purely human way:

Let no one think me a weak one, feeble-spirited,
A stay-at-home, but rather just the opposite,
One who can hurt my enemies and help my friends;
For the lives of such persons are most remembered.
(Medea, 807-810)

Euripides recognized this solution to the problem of a Heliade who
murders her own children. And what an effective solution it is! But
were there grounds for it also in cult, where Medea was an infanticide
before she ever appeared on stage? Euripides himself draws attention
to the fact that the people of Corinth celebrated "a holy feast and sacrifice / Each year for ever to atone for the blood guilt" (lines 1382-1383),
and he also indicates the place of burial where that celebration took
place: in the holy precinct of Hera Akraia on Acrocorinthus. He uses
a word here, *"tele,"* that implies a mystical festival. A later author,
Philostratus, compares it in his *Heroikos* to the ecstatic lamentations
in the mysteries. At one point he even drops the name Adonis, who was
similarly lamented.

About the course of the celebration we know only that annually
seven boys and the same number of girls were brought to the temple of
Hera, where they had to spend the entire year — as though in exile or

30

death. We still have the mythologem on which this was based. For a time after her children were born, Medea concealed them in the temple of Hera. As the mythologem was told in its late form, she believed that this would make the children immortal, but when Jason discovered his wife's unusual behavior he divorced her. This sort of immortalizing by concealment was, therefore, not a harmless act on the part of Medea. The repetition of this practice through the symbolic sacrifice of fourteen boys and girls, the mystical lamentation for the dead, and the pronounced funereal character of the whole festival does not bode well. The only thing on Greek soil that can be compared to this sacrifice is the offering of Athenian maidens and youths who, in the same numbers as in Corinth, were sent to the labyrinth of Crete where they were devoured by the Minotaur.

Other mythological analogies also show up. Once before in the family history of Helios' granddaughter there was that ancestor who allowed his children to disappear immediately after their births: it was Kronos, who devoured his sons. Such practices seem to be right at home in that mythological sphere whose center is occupied by the Sun. The Minotaur, who also had the other name Asterios or Asterion ("the starry") and who devoured the Athenian children, was a son of Helios' daughter, Pasiphaë. Associated with the labyrinth, also, is the name of Pasiphaë's daughter, Ariadne, the grandchild of Helios. The similarity and simultaneous contrast between the images of Medea and Ariadne is stressed by Apollonius of Rhodes when he has his Jason hear the story of the Cretan princess and immediately thereafter has Medea speak the most deeply shocking words of the epic: "Ariadne and I are – not the same!"

MEDEA

Medea is the anti-Ariadne: rather than leading the newly dead back to life like Ariadne does, she leads the newly born back to death. In the middle of Cretan coins on which the labyrinth is represented, there can occasionally be seen a crescent moon rather than either the Minotaur or the suggestion of his face. Seven is a lunar number: seven days signifies a quarter moon: twice seven signifies the moon's waxing or waning. The annual repetition of the Corinthian festival prohibits any thought of a simple imitation of the moon's darker side, this must at the same time be connected to a reference to the sun. The murderous, which was represented in Hera's temple on Acrocorinthus by imitating the disappearing children of Medea, belonged most certainly to a complex context, as the astral mythologists were inclined to believe. In Medea herself there appears a weaving together of the astral and the human. But still we have not proceeded far enough to be able to define her place in the great fabric that is woven out of the existences of Sun and man.

In the Corinthian cult she was a child-concealer, which is merely a milder expression for child-murderer. What turned out to be the case with this murder of children was similar to the murder of the brother: the disappearance was followed by a reappearance. Did this take place under the auspices of Medea or of another Goddess? Always we have found her engaged only in carrying out a murderous act, even if, as in the case of her brother, this served the renewal of the eternally living. Her's is the place of dismemberment, of cutting up and dispersing the living, of murder. But we have also found that she is connected to other Goddesses. On Acrocorinthus it was to Hera. There, too, she was supposed to have founded the temple of Aphrodite. To Apollonius of Rhodes she appeared as the double of the Moon Goddess. And for him, as for the whole of antiquity, she is above all a priestess of Hecate. Perhaps through these Goddesses, or through one or another of them, we can come to know something more about Medea.

Hecate's whole being expresses something lunar, and for Euripides she is Medea's household Goddess. It is Hecate, along with Themis, whom the abandoned one, in her address to "Mistress Artemis," calls upon to witness her oath. The "far away" Goddess (this is the meaning of the name "Hecate"), who chose crossroads as her place of wandering and appearing and who circles around wolfishly in the manner of wild dogs, takes the place in Medea's home of Hestia, the hearth Goddess:

> —I swear it by her, my mistress,
> Whom most I honor and have chosen as partner,
> Hecate, who dwells in the recesses of my hearth —

is how Medea swears her oath in Euripides' play. Corresponding to this in Apollonius is Medea's continual stopping over in the temple of Hecate and acting as her priestess. Hecate was her teacher, and from her she received the knowledge of enchanting herbs and learned how to prepare poisons and antidotes. Medea's sorcery is more a science, that of Circe more an art. Hecate commands the secret knowledge that is not Apollonic; in her the lunar displays its understanding of the most secret exits and entries, of life's origin and its termination.

This accounts for the dominant tradition regarding Medea's mother. There is the possibility that the siblings Aietes and Circe were originally also a married couple and that Medea, under the name of Cassiphone ("the brother-killer"), was a daughter of Circe, but this never became the classical view. Sophocles recognizes Neaira, whose name is of the new moon, as the wife of Aietes, or perhaps it was only as the mother of the murdered brother Apsyrtos-Phaethon. In Apollonius, too, his mother is different from Medea's. There she is called Asterodeia, "she who wanders about either as a star or among the stars." For the entire tradition that became dominant, Medea's mother has the unambiguous name Idyia or Eidyia, "she who knows.' This name is appropriate for the moon, if it is looked at in its Hecate aspect. If Hecate is reckoned as the mother of Medea, it only signifies the expression of something which, in all its essential features, has long since been established.

Aphrodite, whom we encountered at the essential core of Circe, seizes Medea as though from the outside; she puts a charm on her. Euripides and the epic poets preoccupy themselves with explaining their heroine's passionate connection to Jason. And it is a thoroughly significant invention when in the work of Valerius Flaccus, who was the Roman reviser of the argonauts' voyage, Aphrodite appears in the form of Circe. Yet it was not only the later poets, but also Pindar who depicted in detail Aphrodite's invasion. Pindar's account is especially graceful in highlighting the solar features of the love magic which she employs against the moonlike, wily young woman: for the first time — to paraphrase this passage from the fourteenth Pythian Ode — the Mistress of the sharpest arrow, the Goddess born on Cyprus, brought forth from Olympus down to earth among mankind the colorful wryneck, the bird of delirious love, inextricably bound up in the circle of a four-pointed sun-wheel, and taught Jason the art of entreating, which is also the art

34

of oath-taking, so that Medea would lose the timidity she had in front of her parents and that the longing for Greece would strike and pursue her, the shining one, with the lash of Peitho, the servant of Aphrodite and the Goddess of persuasion . . .

What Pindar relates is a genuine mythologem of origin. Aphrodite transferred solar sorcery to earth so that the lunar grandchild of Helios would succumb to the Sun-hero Jason, enchanted by his powers. We are led to the more general reasons for Medea's fate, however, only through her connection to the Goddess who, for Pindar as well, is the propelling force behind the voyage of the Argonauts and who, as the later epic poets put it expressly, is the mover of Aphrodite – Hera. Even in the *Odyssey* Hera's love for Jason is known. As an expansion of this, there is the Corinthian story that Zeus loved Medea, but out of loyalty to Hera she rejected him. All of this bondedness between the two Goddesses – the parallelism of their relation to Jason and the unity of their interests as revealed on Acrocorinthus even in a cultic community – must have reasons more profound than merely poetic.

A cultic community, such as that of Hera and Medea on Acrocorinthus, is conceivable only on the basis of an essential relationship, of an essential similarity between the two deities or between their mutual fulfillments. Medea, the helper of Jason who avenges his adultery through infanticide, corresponds to Hera, the helper of Jason and the guardian of marriage, precisely at the key point where Euripides recognized the solution to her problem. He represented her under the sign of the Corinthian cultic community, as though seen through Hera. He does this without especially emphasizing the connection of this barbaric grandchild of the Sun to the great Olympian Goddess. It is a most remarkable relationship, whose basis in the nature of the two Goddesses should also perhaps be kept secret. From the standpoint of the Olympian religion, it must in fact have seemed odd for the murderous Medea to embody the precepts of the lofty domain of power that was Hera's.

Compared to the Medea of Euripides, the Medea of Apollonius does this in a less gruesome though equally forceful way. The situation that arises as the precepts of Hera are supposed to be realized in the seduction of Medea despite the invasion of Aphrodite would turn out to be almost comical were it not understood from the standpoint of the marriage Goddess. Unlike Persephone, Medea is not abducted. She runs after Jason, whom she has helped out of love for him. When the fleeting Argonauts are overtaken by the Colchians in the land of the Phaeaces, Medea implores Arete, the queen of the Phaeaces, not to deliver her over to her pursuers and to her father. Arete tries to persuade her husband, King Alkinoos, to follow this course. They discuss the serious state of affairs with one another privately during the night. Alkinoos reaches his decision: if Medea is presently the wife of Jason, she will not be returned. If, however, she is still an unmarried young woman, she must return to Aietes. With this resolve, the King falls asleep. The queen gets out of her side of the bed and sends the message to Jason.

Only then is the wedding night of Medea celebrated, now with utmost dispatch. The issue, therefore, is neither a maiden's abduction nor a wild love affair, but rather marriage, which should have been consummated in the home of Jason's parents. That was the intention of both of them. But now they are overcome by necessity, by the

36

decision of Alkinoos. The coerciveness in this situation cannot be easily surmounted, although the poet does everything he can to have them forget it. The cave of Macris, a divine nurse of Dionysus, is chosen for the wedding celebration. On the marriage couch gleams the golden fleece, the Sun-ram's pelt, whose luster fills the scampering nymphs with sweet desire. They bring the flowers which were sent by Hera. And the heroes sing the wedding song, accompanied on the lute by Orpheus. In this manner Hera honors her favorite, and thus, too, she and her world — the world of marriage with its precepts — is honored.

How, then, should the Acrocorinthian cultic community of these two Goddesses be evaluated? What should we make of it that Medea, a barbaric representative of the Hera world, and her gloomy cult found acceptance in the sacred precinct of Zeus' spouse? Did she first come there with the saga of the argonauts' journey and with Jason, the favored hero of Hera? The barbarism of the Medea cult always remained conscious to the Corinthians. The children of Medea, who were honored through the sacrifice of their own children, were named the "half barbarians." Had that holy precinct belonged originally only to Hera, the noble Olympian Goddess, there would have been little prospect that these children of Jason would have been accepted there. Two things speak against such an assumption: the close connection of Medea — and not of the Olympian Hera — to Helios, whose presence defines the cultic atmosphere of Acrocorinthus, and the tradition itself.

Archaic Hellas knew several different mythologems concerning the original distribution of the world and the apportionment of realms and lands to the various deities. Only a few of these stories have been preserved. "People tell us old legends," runs such a mythologem in Pindar; "when Zeus and the immortals divided the earth among themselves, Rhodes was not yet visible on the mirror of the sea; the island was still hidden in the salty depths. And as Helios was not present, nobody assigned him his share. And so it happened that the pure God was left without a land of his own . . ." Almost! As Zeus is about to reapportion the land for the sake of the forgotten one, Helios spies a land rising up from the floor of the sea, and he chooses it: it is the island of Rhodes.

No other story could depict more impressively the position of Helios on the periphery of the Zeus-dominated pantheon. The Corinthians obviously held a different world-image, in which the Sun God played a decisive role. According to their tradition, which was expanded by the epic poet Eumelos and after him also by an old prose narrative, Helios apportioned his part of the world in such a way that one of his sons, Aietes, received what was for the Corinthians certainly the center of the world, namely Corinth itself. Only later did Aietes retreat to Colchis, which lies at the eastern edge of the world. For this reason his daughter Medea could later rightfully rule over Corinth, Jason being recognized only "for her sake" as her "fellow ruler." As the Corinthians understood it, it was not a matter of a Hellene introducing a barbarian, an alien Goddess, from the Orient into the world of Acrocorinthian cult; rather, the strange image of Medea was originally at home there as the daughter of a son of Helios and as queen, and she legitimated her Hellenic spouse.

Translated into a directly religious view, this tradition means that Acrocorinthus was regarded as the Aia of Aietes, as a land of the Sun, but hovering up in the air rather than at the world's edge. Every spot in the antique world where different holy shrines were united to form a provincially connected cultic sphere is a mythological land: it expresses an aspect of the world — sometimes a very complicated one, but always a meaningful one — just like a mythologem in its several variations. On Acrocorinthus there was created a heavenly, transcendent world, a spaceless and timeless realm of the Sun, which could rest at the mid-point as well as be displaced to the edge: an aspect of the world, in that the world's wholeness can be observed from the viewpoint of its genesis as though from a source that lies beyond the world.

In our earlier reflection on Circe, the Acrocorinthian world of genesis was revealed under the sign of Aphrodite. Now we see that this transcendent world owns at least one more aspect, which is both associated with the Sun and yet is far less solar than lunar. Its two sides, which mutually complete one another, come into view. Yet it is not a matter of life standing on the one side and death on the other, but rather Aphrodite here and Hera there. Both sides have to do with realms and mysteries of being that cannot possibly be expressed fully in a single word or even in the compound "life-and-death."

Pre-Greek cultures believed they could grasp such mysteries better through heavenly events, through the vicissitudes of the stars, while the Greeks preferred human forms. For the representatives of both kinds of world-view, human existence was rooted in transcendent astral being — in Uranos and Gaia, as the Greeks expressed it. With C. F. Meyer, or before him J.-J. Rousseau speaking of his own parents, they could say of the Sun and the whole heavenly company: *"Tels furent les auteurs de mes jours"* — "These were the authors of our days." It was however not the moon itself

as Goddess that appeared to the Greeks in a mythologem expressing the
terrifying mysteries about the source of our "days" — rather it was a Medea.

Yet even the Titaness, which is what Medea always remained, did not
satisfy the Greek claim on a level of solution to the problems and paradoxes
of existence as noble and pure as that represented by the Olympian images
of deity. Like the Sun, his granddaughter too had to become a part of the
Olympian order. Hera stepped in beside her barbaric, or at least archaic,
predecessor and surrounded her with the sanctity of her own world. This
took place on the basis of an already existing essential affinity, which
helped to solve the riddle of Medea, just as the Aphroditean element in
the essential core of Circe facilitated the understanding of this daughter of
the Sun. To a certain extent, both Medea and Circe are merely preliminary
stages, and we should count them as such. The higher stages are named
Hera and Aphrodite.

III. A P H R O D I T E

The Golden One

That golden disposition in the feminine, which is the object
of these reflections; that joy-creating characteristic of all the Sun's kin,
which seemed to spring up not only from the paternal Sun God but also
from the queenly nature of the Sun's wife and the Sun's mother – this
we have encountered in the nature of the Sun's daughter, Circe. It was
her Aphroditean enchantment. The same sun-like magic had to be connected to Medea, herself ensnared and enveloped by it, in order for Jason
to have been attracted and bound to her, and she to him. When we consider
this grand-daughter of the Sun under the aspect of Hera, an Olympian
Goddess who reveals much less her own Titanic-astral background and much
more the idea that has become intimately entangled in human form, we can
recognize another presupposition of that drive for oneness and of that
revengefulness at being separated which are characteristic of Medea. This
presupposition is halfness, one of Hera's aspects.

It is part of the profundity of Greek mythology that among its
images something that seems to be purely human, fundamental partialness,

41

appears as a Goddess. Since this is a characteristic of a Great Goddess, one thinks not of accidental partialness but rather of a meaningful plural form. In Hera, feminine being is shown as something that remained half not just by accident. This primal femininity can be represented in the same phases as an independently enduring, eternal form of being. The same pertains to the primal maiden, who is mother in Demeter and reborn in Kore. Within her own circle, Demeter became mother only in order to reappear in her daughter as the eternal, imperishable Ur-Kore, *the* maiden. Considered in this way, even motherhood is related to femininity as to a form of being that possesses its value and status in itself rather than getting it from a function such as 'fertility.' To assign 'fertility' as the singular meaning of a Goddess is possible only in the sense of a concept which recognizes woman merely as a function, but not as essential being.

Even the sovereign feminine circle of Demeter does not exist all by itself within the world fabric made up of all forms of being. It is invaded by the masculine as by an enemy force — by an attacker, robber, and conqueror — and this has a voice even within the totally self-enclosed feminine. Under the sign of Hera, this same circle remains completely round, and yet opens to appeal, in all of its phases, to the masculine. It does not recognize itself as something partial that in and for itself can have no meaning, but rather it represents itself as a halfness that at the same time is filled with meaning. In this case, halfness signifies the relation of one whole to another which corresponds to it. In Hera this relatedness of feminine being, seen as a circle or track, is just as exclusive as is the self-enclosed relatedness of the same circle in the fate of Demeter and her daughter. Demeter became a mother in order to become herself again.

Similarly Hera, who renews herself in Hebe, was, under other circumstances, the mother of Hephaistos, Ares, and Typhon. This she was not on account of selfless maternal fertility, but rather on account of her nature, which is partialness and precisely for this reason craves the power that every wholeness possesses.

Neither Medea nor Hera is 'queen' just on account of being partial. The queen of the underworld, the raped and rediscovered Demeter-Kore has this title in a genuine way, yet she is not partial. In Vergil she is called *"Iuno inferna,"* the "underworld Juno," and she is the *"domina Ditis,"* "Mistress of the King of the Underworld," but he is not termed her "Master," but rather her uncle, her "patruus," a relation that refers back to the rape and most likely also to the founding of the kingdom. It refers back to the founding of the kingdom in that the robbing of the maiden was the first death, the first postulate of the kingdom of the dead. Persephone and Hades do not mutually complete one another. Both imply the same realm, Hades much more impersonally than the mysterious, yet much more defined, image of his queen. We also know that one approaches her, the not-to-be-named, ineffable Maiden, the *Arretos Kura* of the Mysteries, with a golden branch, as she at once receives the gold of our life, preserves it, and also returns it . . . . And she, who receives from everyone the gold that comes from father Helios, which without her would scatter like worthless dust, is also queen. Does this primal form of the feminine reveal itself only in protective reception? In the arrest of pulverizing Titanic violence? Where is the idea of the Basile (or Basileia) revealed to us?

Basileia appears as a particular divine person in a late mythological account, in a creation of Dionysios Skytobrachion in the second century B.C.

APHRODITE

The material itself was not his invention: neither the primal king Uranos; nor his wife, the primal mother Titaia, later called Ge, the "earth"; nor her children, the Titans. From Dionysios Skytobrachion originates only the assertion that this has to do with the stories of the Atlantians about their earlier kings and later Gods. He was probably also the one who, in this Atlantian archaic history, turned a Titaness, the eldest of the children of Uranos and Titaia, into two persons: Basileia and Rhea. He depicts Basileia as though she were the Near-Eastern Great Mother. This figure, Rheia Kybele, in fact belongs among the Goddesses who in their cults were worshipped as "queens." Yet Dionysios, too, remains faithful to the archetypal image of that "queen" to whom our initial reflections led us, when he relates that Basileia, the first Titaness, was the wife of Hyperion and through him became the mother of Helios and Selene.

Nor is it a brand new revelation — rather sooner an emergence out of unclassical folk mythology — when the image of Basileia appears on the stage of old Attic comedy. In the *Birds* of Aristophanes, Prometheus, the enemy of the Gods who is familiar with their secrets, advises Pisthetairos that he should demand Basileia as wife from the distressed king of the Gods, Zeus. Through marriage to this most beautiful divine maiden, one would receive lordship over the whole world. The word "Basileia," differently accented, would commonly mean "kingdom." The nuptial scene at the end of the play, an enthronement of the new world ruler Pisthetairos, does not depend only on a word-play but rather on the idea which we recognized at the end of our reflections on father Helios: the kingdom comes from the queen.[1] Listen to how the world-ruling pair is greeted by the Aristophanian Chorus (as translated by Benjamin Bickley Rogers):

44

APHRODITE

Back with you! out with you!
                    off with you! up with you!
Flying around
Welcome the Blessed with blessedness crowned.
O! O! for the youth and the beauty. O!
Well hast thou wed for the town of the Birds.

Great are the blessings, and mighty, and wonderful,
Which through his favor our nation possesses.
Welcome them back, both himself and Miss Sovereignty,
Welcome with nuptial and bridal addresses.

Mid just such a song hymenaean
Aforetime the Destinies led
The King of the thrones empyréan,
The Ruler of Gods, to the bed
Of Hera his beautiful bride.
Hymen, O Hymenaeus!

The situation in which the Goddess Basileia appears in the flesh is that of the bride-brought-home; the festival in which she is present is the wedding. Even today in the Greek church's wedding ceremony the bridal pair is crowned, and the King of the *Song of Songs* and his beloved are remembered. Specialists of Syrian folk song found parallels to this in wedding songs where every bridegroom appears as king and every bride as queen, where too this rank derives immediately from the nuptial joy of this specific event. The fulfillment is itself the rulership, mutual rulership, not over subjects but rather in a natural, self-sufficient sovereignty . . .

For the Greeks, the world-rulership of Zeus is nothing else than the expansion of such nuptial rulership; it is founded through genuine weddings.

APHRODITE

The first wedding of Zeus, that to the Goddess Themis, the bearer of all the primal laws of Mother Earth, is described in one of Pindar's Odes: "First of all the Fates led good-counseling Themis, the Heavenly, in a golden chariot from the springs of Okeanos up to the holy summit of Olympus on shimmering streets to be the very first wife of Redeemer Zeus . . ." The wedding that sealed the rulership of the world was, however, clearly the one to Hera: the archetype of the Basileia wedding, upon which Aristophanes drew, is the archetype of the Greek wedding, inasmuch as the theme of rape is not predominant in it. Accordingly, Hera, in her nuptial fulfillment, could present us with the primal form of the queen.

How she does this is shown in Homer. In Book XIV of the *Iliad,* the tactical situation of the Greeks, protégés of Hera, is ominous. Giving anxious assistance, Poseidon, who among the Gods is fraternally disposed toward her, inspired the discouraged Greeks with new courage. Yet this alone would be of no real help. The wife and sister of Zeus steps to center stage. The poet devotes nearly the whole book to her action and her epiphany, which is nothing less than the preparation and consummation of a wedding, the repetition of her "Holy Wedding" to Zeus. Like the Gods themselves in Homer, divine "Time" is here freed from the calendrical system and displayed in spontaneous appearance. We must read the whole of the golden scene. I venture to call it such, since even though it is the greatest Hera scene it stands under the sign of that Goddess who for Homer is *the* golden one: Aphrodite.

> Now Hera, she of the golden throne, standing on Olympos' horn, looked out with her eyes, and saw at once how Poseidon, who was her very brother and her lord's brother, was bustling

about the battle where men win glory, and her heart was happy.
Then she saw Zeus, sitting along the loftiest summit
on Ida of the springs, and in her eyes he was hateful.
And now the lady ox-eyed Hera was divided in purpose
as to how she could beguile the brain in Zeus of the aegis.
                                            (Book XIV, 153-160)

Hera's epithet is *"boopis,"* the "cow-eyed." Sacred herds of cattle are owned
by all of those Greek deities who belonged to the Sun's kinship in pre-Greek
cults. Hera's herds were in Argos, and for Homer she still always gazes with
the eyes that once gazed after the Sun-bull.

And to her mind this thing appeared to be the best counsel,
to array herself in loveliness, and go down to Ida,
and perhaps he might be taken with desire to lie in love with her
next her skin, and she might be able to drift an innocent
warm sleep across his eyelids, and seal his crafty perceptions.
She went into her chamber, which her beloved son Hephaistos
had built for her, and closed the leaves in the door-posts snugly
with a secret door-bar, and no other of the gods could open it.
There entering she drew shut the leaves of the shining door, then
first from her adorable body washed away all stains
with ambrosia, and next annointed herself with ambrosial
secret olive oil, which stood there in its fragrance beside her,
and from which, stirred in the house of Zeus by the golden
       pavement,
a fragrance was shaken forever forth, on earth and in heaven.
When with this she had annointed her delicate body
and combed her hair, next with her hands she arranged the
       shining
and lovely and ambrosial curls along her immortal
head, and dressed in an ambrosial robe that Athene

had made her carefully, smooth, and with many figures upon it,
and pinned it across her breast with a golden brooch, and circled
her waist about with a zone that floated a hundred tassles,
and in the lobes of her carefully pierced ears she put rings
with triple drops in mulberry clusters, radiant with beauty,
and, lovely among goddesses, she veiled her head downward
with a sweet fresh veil that glimmered pale like the sunlight.
Underneath her shining feet she bound on the fair sandals.

(Book XIV, 161-186)

It is not a common costume that is described here. To appreciate it in
all its detail, we place beside it the corresponding description from the great
Homeric Hymn to Aphrodite. There the love Goddess, herself in love,
prepares himself for the consummate encounter with Anchises (as translated
by Charles Boer):

And when she saw
him, Aphrodite, lover of laughter, she
loved him, and a terrifying desire seized
her heart.

She went away
to Cyprus, and entered her fragrant
temple at Paphos, where she has a precinct
and a fragrant altar. After going inside
she closed the bright doors, and the
Graces gave her a bath, they oiled her
with sacred olive-oil, the kind that the
gods always have on, that pleasant ambrosia
that she was perfumed with. Having put on
all her beautiful
clothing, and having ornamented herself

APHRODITE

in gold, Aphrodite, lover of laughter,
hurried away to Troy, leaving sweet-smelling
Cyprus, quickly cutting a path through
the clouds high up.

(The Hymn to Aphrodite, I)

On Mount Ida she was accompanied by wild animals — we remind
ourselves of this epiphany — and stepped before Anchises in the form of
an unwed young woman:

> . . . Anchises saw her and he
> marvelled at her, he was astonished by
> her form, and size, and by her expensive
> clothes. She wore a robe that was brighter
> than a fire-flash, and she had on spiral
> ringlets, and bright ornaments,
> and necklaces around her delicate neck
> that were very beautiful, and lovely, and
> golden, and finely wrought, shining like
> the moon on her delicate breasts, and
> astonishing.

(The Hymn to Aphrodite, I)

And how is she clothed when in her first epiphany, her birth from
the sea, she comes to Cyprus?

> In their own fillets of gold
>   the Hours
>   received her
>   happily
> and happily
>   put the ambrosial garments
>   around her.

49

APHRODITE

On her immortal head
    they placed a crown
        that was carefully made,
            beautiful and in gold,
and in the pierced lobes of her ears
    they placed
    flowers of copper
        and precious gold.
On her delicate neck
    and her silver-white breasts
        they arranged
        necklaces of gold . . .

                      (*The Hymn to Aphrodite,* II)

Hera puts on the garments of her epiphany and wedding all by herself; neither Charities nor Horae, who are otherwise coordinated with her in cult or for cultic presentations, assist her. It is just as it was in the original solitude, beyond the world, where her first wedding with Zeus took place. According to Pindar, the first bride of Zeus, Themis, was led for her wedding from the springs of Okeanos up to Olympus; it is significant that Hera stayed "down" at Okeanos' place (several different modes of expression indicate this as the location) —

Where the Lord of the Ocean
denies the voyagers further sailing,
and fixes the solemn limit of Heaven
which Giant Atlas upholds.
There the streams flow with ambrosia
by Zeus's bed of love,
and holy earth, the giver of life,
Yields to the Gods rich blessedness.

                      (*Hippolytus,* lines 744-751)

APHRODITE

This is how a song of the Chorus in Euripides' *Hippolytus* embellishes that otherworldly "place" (as rendered in the translation of David Grene). Another feature of this mythologem is significant: after this the earth, in Hera's honor, produced the tree with the golden apples of the Hesperides, or it was Hera herself who gave this golden wedding present to Zeus. It is as though the primal wedding ran its entire course under the sign of the Sun God returning home to his queen!

How much cooler, though, the luster of Hera's bridal outfit than the finery of Aphrodite! The breasts of the Cyprian Goddess shine for us silvery as the moon, probably uncovered in the fashion of the Cyprian women's bosom. From the Homeric Hymn we learn that this remarkable costume represented a clear association to the moon. Otherwise Aphrodite is decked out in golden jewelry. Hera's brooch, which pins her dress at the bosom, is also golden, but her veil is "pale" – literally "white" – "like the sunlight." Her zone, too, unlike that of Circe, is not golden. Similarly characteristic of her were the "many figures" on her robe, the *"daidale"*: the fourteen dolls, which got burned up after one of her great festivals, the "Daidala," were named after this kind of artistically designed fabric. (Fourteen is also the number of Juno's nymphs in Vergil and the number of children sacrificed to Medea.) We can see the veil in that famous relief of Selinus, where Zeus is shown approaching his bride.

> Now, when she had clothed her body in all this loveliness,
> she went out from the chamber, and called aside Aphrodite
> to come away from the rest of the gods, and spoke a word
> to her:
> 'Would you do something for me, dear child, if I were to
> ask you?

51

APHRODITE

Or would you refuse it? Are you forever angered against me
because I defend the Danaans, while you help the Trojans? '
Then, with false lying purpose the lady Hera answered her:
'Give me loveliness and desirability, graces
with which you overwhelm mortal men, and all the immortals.
Since I go now to the ends of the generous earth, on a visit
to Okeanos, whence the gods have risen, and Tethys our mother
who brought me up kindly in their own house, and cared for me
and took me from Rheia, at that time when Zeus of the wide
    brows
drove Kronos underneath the earth and the barren water.
I shall go to visit these, and resolve their division of discord,
since now for a long time they have stayed apart from each other
and from the bed of love, since rancour has entered their
    feelings.
Could I win over with persuasion the dear heart within them
and bring them back to their bed to be merged in love with
    each other
I shall be forever called honoured by them, and beloved.'
Then in turn Aphrodite the laughing answered her:
'I cannot, and I must not deny this thing that you ask for,
you, who lie in the arms of Zeus, since he is our greatest.'
She spoke, and from her breasts unbound the elaborate,
    pattern-pierced
zone, and on it are figured all beguilements, and loveliness
is figured upon it, and passion of sex is there, and the whispered
endearment that steals the heart away even from the thoughtful.
She put this in Hera's hands, and called her by name and spoke
    to her:
'Take this zone, and hide it away in the fold of your bosom.
It is elaborate, all things are figured therein. And I
    think

52

whatever is your heart's desire shall not go unaccomplished.'
So she spoke, and the ox-eyed lady Hera smiled on her
and smiling hid the zone away in the fold of her bosom.
So Aphrodite went back into the house, Zeus' daughter,
while Hera in a flash of speed left the horn of Olympos
and crossed over Pieria and Emathia the lovely
and overswept the snowy hills of the Thracian riders
and their uttermost pinnacles, nor touched the ground
with her feet.

(Book XIV, 187-223)

In the original text nothing is said about "magic": the *"kestos himas,"* Aphrodite's zone, is many-colored, like the world which for lovers glistens in an otherwise never experienced power of color, full of enchanting surprises. "Magic" must here be understood in the purely natural sense, as the primal magic of love, as that Aphroditean magic which is also the fundamental sorcery of Circe. Even if deceiving in its transient splendor – deceiving like happiness, which for us mortals contains eternity only in its depths and not in its duration – that magic is nevertheless warm and genuine, like the rays of the sun. It is the warmth and truth of passion that shine through Aphrodite's nature, as sunlike gold shines through her whole appearance. In this respect, too, Hera seems cool. Not that she is without passion. But in her we recognize with a shudder a different, a calculating, passion. Hera knows that she needs Aphrodite's magic, the purely atmospheric magic with which Circe acquainted us, if she is to celebrate, and to rule over, a wedding. In no way does a wedding simply blossom, nor a queen simply rise up out of mere halfness. Hera possesses something beyond that. She takes Hypnos, Sleep, along in her service and strides forth from preparation to consummation.

53

APHRODITE

But Hera light-footed made her way to the peak of Gargaros
on towering Ida. And Zeus who gathers the clouds saw her,
and when he saw her desire was a mist about his close heart
as much as on that time they first went to bed together
and lay in love, and their dear parents knew nothing of it.
He stood before her and called her by name and spoke to
    her: 'Hera,
what is your desire that you come down here from Olympos?
And your horses are not here, nor your chariot, which you
    would ride in.'

Then with false lying purpose the lady Hera answered him:
'I am going to the ends of the generous earth, on a visit
to Okeanos, whence the gods have risen, and Tethys our
    mother,
who brought me up kindly in their own house, and cared for me.
I shall go to visit these, and resolve their division of discord,
since now for a long time they have stayed apart from each other
and from the bed of love, since rancour has entered their
    feelings.
In the foothills by Ida of the waters are standing
my horses, who will carry me over hard land and water.
Only now I have come down here from Olympos for your sake
so you will not be angry with me afterwards, if I
have gone silently to the house of deep-sunning Okeanos.'

Then in turn Zeus who gathers the clouds answered her:
'Hera, there will be a time afterwards when you can go there
as well. But now let us go to bed and turn to love-making.
For never before has love for any goddess or woman
so melted about the heart inside me, broken it to submission,
as now: not that time when I loved the wife of Ixion . . .
                (*Iliad,* Book XIV, 292-317)

54

APHRODITE

Here begins the *Iliad's* famous "Leporello list," delivered by Zeus himself. One is not inclined to believe that the intention here is to create an especially comic effect. (We may laugh, in Homer's sense, about the whole divine game, laugh because up there it is play that here below would create incurable wounds . . .) Zeus, who has been enchanted by the miraculous zone, speaks with the passion of love, not however the sort of love that binds and is bound one to another, but rather the sort that is Aphrodite's gold — free of all love's memories and streaming forth impersonally. And it is the paradox of this passion that without paying attention to those memories it believes itself to be the strongest ever in the present moment —

> as now I love you, and the sweet passion has taken hold of me.'
> Then with false lying purpose the lady Hera answered him:
> 'Most honoured son of Kronos, what sort of thing have
>   you spoken?
> If now your great desire is to lie in love together
> here on the peaks of Ida, everything can be seen. Then
> what would happen if some one of the gods everlasting
> saw us sleeping, and went and told all the other immortals
> of it? I would not simply rise out of bed and go back
> again, into your house, and such a thing would be shameful.
> No, if this is your heart's desire, if this is your wish, then
> there is my chamber, which my beloved son Hephaistos
> has built for me, and closed the leaves in the door-posts
>   snugly
> We can go back there and lie down, since bed is your pleasure.'
>
> Then in turn Zeus who gathers the clouds answered her:
> 'Hera, do not fear that any mortal or any god

will see, so close shall be the golden cloud that I gather
about us. Not even Helios can look at us through it,
although beyond all others his light has the sharpest vision.'

So speaking, the son of Kronos caught his wife in his arms,
    There
underneath them the divine earth broke into young, fresh
grass, and into dewy clover, crocus and hyacinth
so thick and soft it held the hard ground deep away from them.
There they lay down together and drew about them a golden
wonderful cloud, and from it the glimmering dew descended.

So the father slept unshaken on the peak of Gargaron
with his wife in his arms, when sleep and passion had stilled him.
                                        (*Iliad,* Book XIV, 328-353)

It is precisely in her character as marriage Goddess that Hera is also
called "Antheia," the "Goddess of blossoms." In this character she sends,
according to Apollonius of Rhodes, nymphs with flowers to the wedding
of Medea and Jason. In this respect, too, she is the granddaughter of her
grandmother, flower-giving Earth. She expresses the darker and cooler, the
chthonic, side of the marriage event; the brighter and warmer side is created
by Aphrodite's magic, that passion which surrounds the divine couple with
golden clouds. This passion is not chthonic, just as Aphrodite, too, is a
heavenly Goddess. It seems to be something that is in itself of royal nature:
a dominant for its own sake — that is, under the sign of Aphrodite, while
for Hera it is a means for gaining dominance — and if anything at all, it is
precisely the gift of a queen .

Aphrodite is as little a "fertility Goddess" as Demeter or Hera. On
Lesbos, where she found a profoundly congenial devotee in the great

APHRODITE

poetess Sappho, there was a river that was called Aphrodisios in her honor. It was said that the women who bathed in it became infertile. To be sure, she does appear as a marriage Goddess. But not in Homer, for whom she rather manifests the liberty that lies in nature as opposed to the exclusiveness of the marriage bond. The poet of the *Iliad* either does not know of, or does not recognize, her marriage to Hephaistos. The Odyssey represents her as an adultress and Hephaistos as the comical cuckolded husband who tries to hold in his net the one who in her pearly escaping is supremely ungraspable. When it is said in the desperate prayer of Penelope that Aphrodite, at the behest of Zeus, had wanted to bring about the "fulfillment," the *"telos,"* of the orphaned daughters of Pandareos in marriage, she did this as the maternal protectress of those young girls.

Marriage has a place in the realm of Aphrodite. She is generally called upon as the "nuptial Goddess of young girls." It is not without good reason that brides and their mothers sacrifice to her before the wedding. In this respect she bears in Sparta, most extraordinarily, the name of another Goddess, as a confining and circumscribing epithet: she is called Aphrodite Hera. The stunning question of Mimnermos, whether there exists even the possibility of life and enjoyment without "golden Aphrodite," whether life without her is still life, counts in an altogether particular way for marriage, precisely because it does not only serve "fertility" but can be *the* high moment for husband and wife. The word "aphrodite" can be used to denote the pleasure of love, just as "hephaistos" can stand for "fire," "demeter" for "grain," "dionysos" for "wine." One may think of this pleasure when Homer (and in his poem especially Paris, who was distinguished by Aphrodite's "desirable gift") names the

57

APHRODITE

Goddess the "Golden," or when Hesiod does not neglect to use this epithet even when he denotes by the name of Aphrodite merely a fruitful love-union.

Under the sign of Aphrodite we are not dealing with something heavy and darkly earthy, with an unconscious dissolution into a state of fusion, but rather with something bright and lucid. The images of Anadyomene rising up out of the depths of the sea, is the transparent purity of complete union become visible. Through Aphrodite the whole world becomes pellucid and thus so brilliant and smiling, because in her the opposites are dissolved into unity, and this unity reveals to every living being the possibility of the same unproblematic — using the current adjective, though said in a more Greek way it would be calm-sealike — situation. Following the mythologem of her birth, as Hesiod presents it, the primal unity which was broken by the bloody deed of Kronos is restored through the fact that the severed male member was received in the sea's maternal lap and there conceived the Great Goddess of love, the only one of the Titanic generation whose mother is not Gaia. Hera carries the wound of the tragic primal event, Aphrodite the healing of it.

Fittingly enough the Cyprian cult of Aphrodite exhibits an hermaphroditic theme: the Goddess was worshipped there also as a God, as Aphroditos. It seems that in this cult the gleam of another star joined the solar and lunar themes to form that heavenly-earthly web of things that arranges existence for man. The position of the honored planet Venus in the Near East, third after the sun and moon, corresponds exactly to the cultic situation of Aphrodite on Acrocorinthus and also to her appearance beside, but apart from, the Titans and Titanesses (those sunlike and moonlike

58

ones) in Hesiod. But for Greek religion, which put great distance between itself and that Titanic-astral background, it remains significant that in later antiquity the attempt was made to ascribe the planet Venus to Hera, even though it is more golden and sunlike than silver and moonlike. The astral pair Zeus and Hera ruled the Olympian world, after the never-forgotten original parental pair Uranos and Gaia and after the Titanic pair Kronos and Rhea: though not identical to sun and moon, they nevertheless corresponded to them at many points. One among others of these is that beside them no third ruling star can maintain an equal position.

This principle was operative as early as Homer, where Aphrodite appears among the daughters of Zeus. The Goddess whom she receives for a mother is left sufficiently mysterious. She is called Dione, a name that belongs to the stem of the word "Zeus" as a feminine form. In Dodona, an extremely ancient cultic location of Zeus, she was his wife. Phonetically her name corresponds not to the Latin "Iuno," but rather more to "Diana," and seems to have the same relation to the moon as all these Goddesses, Diana no less than Juno-Neiaira. In a list of Titans and Titanesses, she is placed next to Theia, the mother of Helios. If it is later asserted that she is the daughter of Theia, she becomes then the sister of the Sun God. Antique theologians probably knew about her lunar character. Whereas in poetic works, she becomes her great daughter Aphrodite and another name for the love Goddess.

Shining in golden purity, Aphrodite, the male-female wholeness, makes pale every sort of partialness. She is present when wholeness emerges from the halves and when the resolved opposites become the indissoluble golden-ness of life. Even though she is not by nature chthonic, she is in harmony

59

with the nocturnal "queen' with whom Helios regains his squandered golden self, reassembled for a new birth. The nocturnal connections of Aphrodite are present in the classical tradition but deeply reserved when they have to do not with the night of love but with the night of death. Nevertheless, it is once disclosed that in Delphi an Aphrodite "of the graves," an *"Epitymbidia,"* was worshipped. Some wonderful artistic monuments in Magna Graecia show us directly how the underworld Goddess Persephone can appear as Aphroditean, and how experientially religious it was intended when the Pythagoreans taught that there are two Aphrodites, a heavenly one and an underworldly one. Aphrodite also has her Persephone aspect, and precisely in the place where this was known, in the south Italian Greek city of Tarent, she was named Queen.

IV. NIOBE

> Ah, Niobe, with eyes how full of pain
> I saw thine image on the roadway scored
> Set between seven and seven thy children slain!
>
> Dante, *Purgatorio,* XII, 37-39

Dante had an easy time of it with the image of Niobe. The image of one who was punished in an exemplary fashion was for him an example of divine justice. Ovid offered him the text,[1] and the relation of the Christian to his God left room for no other result. This presumptuous one, who though merely an earthly queen yet demanded divine worship; who with visible high rank, power, and children elevated herself above the invisible Ones, possessed by the sin of *superbia* — she belonged with her famous, self-inflicted suffering if not in Hell then certainly in Purgatory. And the death of her innocent children was no greater reproach to God's justice than was the slaughter of the infants of Bethlehem.

They also had it easy, these hunters for antiquities who unearthed the statue of Niobe's children, since then much admired, in the Vigna Tomasini near the Lateran Basilica.[2] Their only concern was to discover the whole "story": *trovare tutta la storia.* And among classical scholars there were likewise some who, like those *cavatori* of the 16th century, saw one *storia* of the thousands of ancient stories, a thousand times reproduced.

Jacob Burckhardt did not belong to this group. He took the matter seriously and found it important enough to base his historical critique of the Gods of Greece upon it. "Look at the inconsolable Niobe," he had one of the Olympians say; "we allowed her innocent children to be slain simply in order to create unspeakable grief for their proud mother . . . we were not good, and therefore we must perish."[3] This interpretation does not evade the difficulties. Winckelmann still tries to evade them by wanting to let the monstrousness of mother and children suffering "indescribable fear with deafening sensitivity" disappear in favor of beauty: "Such a situation, where feeling and reflection cease, which is similar to indifference, does not alter a single feature of the image and form, and the great artist could fashion the most exalted beauty exactly as he did in fact fashion it: for Niobe and her daughters are and remain the most exalted ideas themselves."

To the eyes of Winckelmann, which were accustomed to Bernini's Pathetic, even the work of a Scopas, who was most probably the creator of the original Niobe-group,[4] appeared only as the realization of beauty and not as the representation of something horrible and difficult. Let us fix our standpoint there, where that which is so difficult to bear from a human point of view did indeed show itself in the most noble beauty that was ever achieved in Greek art. The throne of Olympian Zeus, the Zeus of Phidias, was decorated with the death of Niobe's daughters and sons.[5] The highest God's image, which the Greeks counted as the most sublime and of which if of anything in Greece it could be said: "The image of God is not an arbitrary product of the 'imagination' but rather a form by means of which

God and man encounter one another"[6] – this image rested upon such scenes. Visible on the two front legs of the throne were the Theban children, stolen by the sphinxes who presumably formed the throne's armrests. Beneath these sphinxes, represented on friezes to both sides of the armrests, as one must assume, one saw Niobe's children: the sons falling to the bow of Apollo, the daughters slain by the arrows of Artemis.

Were they meaningless scenes, chosen as decorations for the throne without purpose and without relation to the God-image? Supposing this were the case; supposing that what was represented as decoration had its meaning not in relation to something supra-individual but rather in a sad story customarily told but really only the particular tale of these hapless, accidentally shot children: would this still have been "decoration"? Socrates, the philosopher of whom it was told that he had earlier been a sculptor's journeyman, takes a different point of view: he directs his eyes to the individual, to the single person, to the single soul with its destiny, its guilt, and its atonement. And in his ideal state, as this is depicted by Plato, he logically had to forbid above all else the story of Niobe as this was presented on stage by Aeschylus.

Was Phidias, then, and Greek art at its classical highpoint in Olympia, still so hard and inhuman, so unfeeling and thoughtless, that in honor of the father of Gods and of human beings the sacrifice of youths and maidens could be represented? For it has nothing to do with just punishment when one considers the fate of Niobe's children and the children of the Thebans, whether it be as the fate of a group of people where the worth of individuals is not even considered, or as the horrible fate of individuals where the individual has the right to ask, why me? At this point Socrates has to brand the appeal to God's power as blasphemy. But even from a pre-Socratic point of view, the power of Zeus, conqueror of Titans and Giants, would not be glorified by the destruction of tender, innocent children! What is made visible in these death scenes is a reference that lies beyond the fate of groups and individuals, from the standpoint of a highly religious, neither moral nor immoral, but rather objective art, something universal, but not for that reason any less horrible or humanly easier to bear. It is the universally human, that famous object of classical art, which is represented not as an abstraction, let alone as an ideal, but rather as a reduction to its core and a condensation to its essence. This is what one could observe in the throne of Zeus: the human condition itself contrasted with the divine in pictures of surrender, as the Theban children were given over the daemon of death and Niobe's children to the angered Deities . . .

Even if she is not visible, Niobe is not to be imagined as absent from her children. It remains questionable whether the image of the mother, whose presence at the scene of the murder would have lent it the character of a punishment scene, was ever represented on the relief. The reference to and the meaning of the death of the children on the throne of Zeus make them into representatives of the human race in contrast to the Gods and makes their mother into the universal mother of mankind. This is para-doxical since Niobe is not separated by any sort of "infinite distance"[7] from Leto, the offended mother of Apollo and Artemis: the mother of humans from the mother of Gods. In all versions of her story she is close to the Gods, whether as daughter of Tantalus or as primordial woman. Even Ovid still allows the Tantalide to brag about her divine descent almost as much as about the number of her children. The tale of her transformation into an

NIOBE

eternally weeping stone in Asia Minor remained for the Greeks an evidence of her originally divine rank: the Great Mother Goddess of Asia Minor was much too closely connected to rocky mountains. Near her location stood Niobe, her stone image right next to it, on Mount Sipylos behind Smyrna. The name "Niobe," too, is from Asia Minor; it has the same characteristic ending as the name of the queen of Troy, "Hekabe," and the same as the Great Mother of the Gods herself who was named not only Kybele but also "Kybebe."

Sophocles hints at this ancient divine rank when he has his Electra call out:

> And Niobe, that suffered all, you, too,
> I count God
> who weeps perpetually
> in her rocky grave.
> (*Electra,* 150-54; translated by David Grene)

Antigone, about to be buried alive, compares herself to Niobe on her way to the stony chamber:

> Pitiful was the death that stranger died,
> our queen once, Tantalus' daughter. The rock
> it covered her over, like stubborn ivy it grew.
> Still, as she wastes, the rain
> and snow companion on her.
> Pouring down from her mourning eyes comes the water that
>   soaks the stone.
> My own putting to sleep as god has planned like hers.
> (*Antigone,* 823-31; translated by Elizabeth Wyckoff)

The Chorus, however, raises its voice against this and honors Niobe as higher:

NIOBE

> God's child and god she was.
> We are born to death.

We have a report that the Cilicians of Asia Minor worshipped Niobe as a Goddess.[8] From whatever source the knowledge of her divinity was fed, whether from the stone image on Sipylus or from her cult in Cilicia, it lived on in Greek tragedy. For this reason it is so significant that Aeschylus, who, as the poetic formulator of the material for the other great shaper of it, stands closest to Phidias, uses Niobe's fate to exemplify the general human condition and not just a punishment. A fragment of his tragedy *Niobe* has been rediscovered on a sheet of papyrus, and there this is clearly expressed.[9] The speaker is a God.[10] His words are directed to the audience, as Niobe sits dumbly for three days at the grave of her children. Which God could this be? Perhaps this is illuminated by the wisdom of the words, which transcend both the divine and the human, and also by a vase painting which brings together the participants in the tragedy.[11] There, in the uppermost sectors elevated above the earthly events, one sees Leto, Apollo, and Artemis on the one side, Zeus and Hermes on the other. The messenger of the Gods played a role in more than just one tragedy by Aeschylus. It is he who also could have been responsible for the teaching which Socrates rejects in Plato's *Republic:*

> I tell you, since you are not ignorant:
> The God of death creates the cause
> When he wishes to bring a house to destruction.

The cause for Hermes' appearance is probably to be thought of as follows: the ghastly unspoken suffering of Niobe, which had already lasted for three days, disturbed the Gods, and Zeus then sent his messenger to her. Another

66

time, also, when Demeter was mourning her daughter and refused to take any nourishment, the Gods were dismayed and did everything to bring the grief and fasting to an end. The story of Niobe is told in the last Book of the *Iliad* precisely because her fasting also came to an end:

> But she remembered to eat when she was worn out with weeping.[12] (Book XXIV, 613)

Homer then refers also to the version of her being turned to stone in the mountain of Sipylus. The circumstance that one also knew of a comforted Niobe allows us to place her beside a great Goddess, Demeter. But the more the suffering of Niobe proves to be the suffering of a Goddess, the more significant becomes its character as punishment. For the mistake — whatever it was — was but small in relation to the consequence. To be subjected to such a punishment is a human element which separates this suffering from the grief of Demeter and relates it to the sort of suffering to which Aeschylus devoted two tragedies: the suffering of Prometheus.

It is remarkable how even late antiquity was still conscious of the relationship between these two mythologems. The dream interpreter Artemidorus, following familiar teaching,[13] divided the stories into three classes: the true, the untrue, and those "which are often told and believed by most." Of these latter, however, he names only two: the story of Prometheus and that of Niobe.[14] Among the murals of the once famous but now deteriorated Columbarium of the Villa Doria Pamfili in Rome there were only two which in spatial arrangement showed complete symmetry:[15] the freeing of Prometheus and the punishment of Niobe. Archeologists demonstrated a point-for-point parallelism and contrast between the two scenes, and one of them was led to state the comparison of Niobe and Prometheus as "primordial images of woman and man in their striving and enduring";[17] a schematic and moralizing anticipation of what forces itself upon us today and what is meant to be more precisely understood in this essay.

An image of the bound Prometheus, with Hercules the liberator looking at him, was also present on the throne of Zeus at Olympia. Only there it corresponded not to the loss of Niobe's children but to the heaven-carrying Atlas. Prometheus and Atlas were the two images that enclosed the archaic world-picture: on the one side the suffering one, on the other the eternally striving. With these two scenes, and otherwise only with scenes of human heroics, Panaenus, the brother of Phidias, decorated the balustrade that ran around the throne.[18] Altogether differently constituted is the evidence which convinces us that Niobe belongs as primordial woman to the primordial man of the Greeks. In the various different geographical areas of Greece there were different traditions regarding the first man. In Argos he was called Phoroneus: he founded the first city and first brought fire and sacrificed, like Prometheus.[19] Plato named Niobe along with this Phoroneus as the first living humans prior to the Deucalion Flood.[20] According to one tradition Niobe was held to be the mother of Phoroneus, according to another his daughter and the first human woman loved by Zeus.[21] In Boeotia the first human was called Alalkomeneus, and Niobe was also mentioned as his wife.[22] There she is better known as the wife of one of the Theban Dioscuroi, the primordial twins Amphion and Zethos.[23]

What is it supposed to signify in Greek mythology that Niobe is a "primordial woman,"[24] "a primordial image of mankind,"[25] "the primordial mother of the human race"?[26] To begin with, it signifies the solution to the paradox which consists in the fact that Niobe is a Goddess and yet also the carrier of the difficult human fate of being severely punished on account of human error. The same was true of Prometheus. He too was a God, one of the oldest Gods, a Titan. And deathless as the Gods, he bore the human condition as something eternal. The Greeks counted only individual persons as mortal; the human form of existence was as eternal for them as the human race itself. If it is to be called a "world," the Greek world with its Gods might be called a "world of human beings."[27] In it the human has its existence, crafty and suffering, immoderately punished because of its cunning. And the human inheres in it so intimately that man can even recognize himself in the heavens. He recognizes himself in the most changeable, the most fickle, of all the heavenly bodies the most implicated in darkness. Prometheus, mankind's representative among the Gods and in the dispute with Zeus, the one who takes the part of man, appears as a nocturnal being connected to the moon − thus is briefly recapitulated what has already been amplified elsewhere.[28]

As a working hypothesis for fellow researchers I will venture a sketch for the possible development of the mythologem of the argument between Prometheus and Zeus, the representative for the race of Gods. In a mytho-historical context, one thinks of it as a story following the type of the familiar African fairytale.[29] "Sun and Moon are real siblings," runs the African mythologem which is told as a fairytale. "They played clever tricks on each other. Moon said to Sun: we want to throw our children into the water. Sun agreed. When the agreed-upon time came, Moon hid its children, searched for white pebbles and put them in a sack. Sun, however, knew nothing about this and really did take all of its children and put them into a sack. So they set out on their way and came to the bank of a river. Moon emptied its pebble-filled sack into the river. Thus was Sun deceived and shook its children into the river . . ." For this reason it has come about that the moon is always accompanied by its children, the stars of the night, while the children of the sun, who had earlier accompanied it also, populate the waters as fishes and feed mankind. Therefore Sun naturally became "angry and attacked Moon . . ."

Hesiod's account in the *Theogony* of the dispute between Zeus and Prometheus repeats the same primordial mythological situation. Two mythological beings who are likewise siblings — for "the beginning of things were the same for Gods and mortal human beings"[30] — undertake a common task. The one is in possession of all-seeing *Nous*, of sun-like understanding. Yet he is tricked by the other one. As punishment this second one is chained to a cliff between heaven and earth.[31] By day his liver — that "dark thing," as Aeschylus literally describes it in his *Prometheus Bound*[32] — is devoured by the eagle of Zeus, by night it grows back again. The situation of the moon "hanging" between heaven and earth, whose darkness sometimes wanes and sometimes waxes, is still present in the suffering of Prometheus, even though the one who is deceived is a spiritual God and the other, the cunning one, is identified with the suffering race of humans. We called the Greek world with its Gods a "human world." It is a divine-human world: even the divine, the more-than-human in it is allowed to appear in human form, and also the human in it, its darker portion, finds its way into such divine images as had their place originally in the heavens. This kind of model makes it understandable for us to see in Prometheus a "primordial man" in what was formerly a "moon-God."

70

NIOBE

But how is Niobe to be understood as "primordial woman"? "Leto and Niobe were once good friends" — thus Sappho began the story of Niobe in a song that has been lost to us:[33] *LATO KAI NIOBA MALA MEN PHILAI ESSAN ETAIRAIS* — but they soon fell into conflict. The whole tradition attributes the reason for the conflict to the number of children. Leto had only two, Apollo and Artemis. There was no question which of the friends should have been the winner. But how terrible the defeat of Niobe! One reads of this in the last book of the *Iliad:*

> ... six sons in the pride of their youth, whom Apollo
> killed with arrows from his silver bow, being angered
> with Niobe, and shaft-showering Artemis killed the daughters;
> because Niobe likened herself to Leto of the fair coloring
> and said Leto had borne only two, she herself had borne many;
> but the two, though they were only two, destroyed all those others.
> Nine days long they lay in their blood, nor was there anyone
> to bury them, for the son of Kronos made stones out of
> the people; but on the tenth day the Uranian gods buried them.[34]
> (Book XXIV, 604-612)

In Homer the number of children is twelve, a Homeric "round" number which is not to be disconnected from its cosmic background, the twelve months of the solar year; it is also a number of completeness, as evidenced in Achilles' sacrifice of twelve youths on the gigantic funeral pyre of Patrocles which had been built up on a quadratic base.[35] Besides the number twelve, the numbers nine and ten play a significant role in Homer's account: for nine days Niobe's slain children have to lie there unburied and only on the tenth are they interred by the celestial Gods, because the people who had seen it were turned to stone.[36] The spreading of petrification among the persons gripped with fright rests on an ancient etymological play on words which derived "people" (*laos*) from "stone" (lãas). It seems that originally it was Niobe's children, not their mother, who were turned to stone, and *that* counted as burial by the Gods. The terrible fate of Niobe's children is related to a specifically defined period of time — a period of victory for Leto, Apollo, and Artemis and a period of mourning for Niobe — the burial on the tenth day signifies a period of terror which encompasses one-third of the triangulated lunar month in the Greek calendar. The most common variants on the number of Niobe's children in the remaining traditions[37] — fourteen, eighteen, nineteen, twenty — can also be understood in relation to units of time, leading to the thought that numbers of days became numbers of children. In the older Greek reckoning of time, the existence of time periods running concurrently seven days and nine days can be established.[38] Both of these time periods can be derived from the sidereal lunar month. This consists of twenty-seven-and-one-half days during which the moon appears: rounded out upwards and divided into quarters, this month yields four weeks of seven days; or rounded out downwards and divided into thirds, it yields three weeks of nine days. The number fourteen, which otherwise also plays a role in Greek cult and myth,[39] indicates the division into quarters, and in this respect the fourteen children of Niobe correspond to a half-month.

The complete lunar month, however, consists of not only the days in which the moon appears but also of the moonless days, and with these it is more than twenty-nine and less than thirty. The number eighteen amounts to two-thirds of the sidereal lunar month, but twenty represents two-thirds of the upwardly rounded-out thirty-day month of the practical Greek calendar, while the number nineteen represents a correction of eighteen in the direction of the actual full lunar month. The time unit underlying all of these numbers is a third of the month, made up of nine to ten days. This unit is reflected in the nine days of Demeter's fasting, or in the fact that Leto's travail lasted nine days[40] and that Apollo was born as Eikadios on the twentieth day of the month, that is on the tenth day of the second third (although according to the other reckoning of time, based on a quarterly division, the birthday of Apollo is the seventh).[41] The *Iliad* (Book I, 53-54) describes a period of Apollo's anger — and of the God in his dark, nocturnal aspect — which lasts nine days and ceases on the tenth. A period of brilliance for Artemis, which is of the same length and ceases on the tenth day, is to be calculated from Greek calendars of Asia Minor: from the entrance of Artemis on the sixth day of the month (Eisiteria) until her exit on the fifteenth, there is the festival of Artemis Apobatieria.[42] The period of Artemis' brilliance is also a happy period for Leto. One reads of it in the *Odyssey*, where the moon has already disappeared from the background, the Gods' epiphany, and only its gleam, as if from out of an invisible source, fills the scene:

> And as Artemis, who showers arrows, moves on the mountains
> either along Taÿgetos or on high-towering
> Erymanthos, delighting in boars and deer in their running,
> and along with her nymphs, daughter of Zeus of the aegis,
> range in the wilds and play, and the heart of Leto is
> gladdened . . . (Book VI, 102-106)

If nine such days and such *nights* belonged to Leto and if she reigned over them with her daughter and her son, the friend with her eighteen, nineteen, or twenty remained all the darker. According to the variant which gave Niobe only fourteen children, it had to do merely with halves: to Leto belonged the lighter and more glorious half, to her rival the darker, more fruitful half teeming with children. Thus Leto appears in her full glory as the mother of the handsome son and also in the symbol of Artemis, the maidenly helper at births, and again brilliantly in the daughter. We also know the darker Leto: the one fleeing in the form of a wolf, threatened and persecuted.[43] But where she was especially worshipped, in Asia Minor, one is allowed to name her, and Artemis as well, a great moon-Goddess in a much more concrete sense than in Greece and to ascribe lord-ship over the period of the full moon to her.

Niobe also appeared to us as "moon-Goddess," but only as the Goddess of the darker half or of the darker two-thirds. Her sphere of power is that of the waning moon, of the growing darkness. Does one recognize here the "primordial woman," the "primordial mother of the human race"? This is what she became precisely because that hemisphere fell to her. How it became hers is told in a story. The tale of this perhaps original failure on Niobe's part is preserved for us by an Athenian painter of the fifth century.[44] A copy of his composition was found painted on marble in Herculaneum. There one sees Leto and Niobe with three other friends playing bones, a game about which more will be said later. The names are inscribed, so we know that the other three bone-game players are called Aglaie, Hilaeira, and Phoibe. One would be eager to know what kind of beings these are, these girls who were allowed to pursue the games of great Goddesses. The presence of Leto elevates the whole group into the sphere of the divine, or at least into that primordial time when there did not yet exist a distance between the divine and the human, not yet a split into two hemispheres.

The names of the three unknown women are illuminating and transparent, and they themselves are delicate and beautiful. They could be the Charites, since Aglaie is, according to Hesiod, one of the three Charites, and her toy, the little bone, was ascribed as an attribute to one of the Charites in Elis.[45] The other two, however, according to their names belong to a different mythological group of sisters. Hilaeira and Phoibe were the names of the two Leucippides who were raped by the Dioscuroi, Castor and Pollux.[46] Arsinoe was also counted as a daughter of Leucippus, and so like the three Charites the Leucippides were three sisters.[47] All three had a specific relation to greater Deities. The two brides of the Dioscuroi, Hilaeira and Phoibe, appeared as closely connected to one another and also as daughters of Apollo.[48] According to Messenian tradition Arsinoe bore Asclepius to Apollo.[49] Only later was it said that Hilaeira had been a priestess of Artemis and Phoibe a priestess of Athene. In Sparta they themselves had a temple, and in Argos their statues stood in the temple of the Dioscuroi.[50] Their names are lunar names. ' Hilaeiro" is an epithet of Selene,[51] a designation of the full moon with the meaning of "mild" and "gracious." "Phoibe," in Hesiod, is the Titaness from whom Leto and her children, Artemis and Phoibus Apollo, descend. But this great Goddess cannot be standing next to Leto and Artemis in the form of a younger girl. "Phoibe" was originally the Moon-Goddess but without a firm geneological specification: therefore, for the Roman poets, Diana bears this name.[52] Hilaeira was coordinated with Artemis, Phiobe with Athene, as priestesses. If one recalls that Athene had her greatest festival in the time of darkness around the new moon, one is able to place the two brides of the Dioscuroi in relation to the phases of the moon such that the darker part falls to Phoibe, the brighter to Hilaeira. If one were able to count a third heroine as a Leucippide, this would make possible the circumstance that the Greeks were used to dividing the lunar month into both two and three phases.

With the Charites the state of affairs is similar, as for example in their cultic relation to the Dioscuroi. These shared a common sanctuary in Sparta,[53] just like the Leucippides did in Argos. Also, the number of Charites varies between two and three. The Spartans worshipped two Charites.[54] They named them Cleta and Phaenna, two names with a clear relation to the Moon-Goddess. She was "Cleta," the "Called," in the time of the new moon.[55] And she was also "Phaenna," the "Brilliant," so named most likely in the brighter portion of the lunar month as she was named "Cleta" in the darker part. The Athenians also had a tradition[56] of two Charites: "Auxo," the "Growing," and "Hegemone," the "One Going On Ahead." "Auxo" is the moon in the first half of the moon: growing and growth-promoting. "Hegemone" is in Sparta and Arcadia an epithet of Artemis,[57] whose meaning is that the waning moon goes ahead of the sun. It gets up before the sun and goes down ahead of it. But usually there are three Charites. They were worshipped in this number in the Boeotian city of Orchomeneos, their famous cultic location. Hesiod knows them as three sisters, while Homer leaves their number indefinite and does not take up in his picture of the world their relation to the moon, just as he also does not with Leto and Artemis. Also the names which Hesiod mentions — Aglaia, Euphrosyne, Thalie — no longer reflect in an original way the three lunar phases. If Pindar prays for the "pure light of the Charites,"[58] he means

76

something more spiritual than moonlight. The poet Antimachus provides the
Charites with parents who are suitable for Moon Goddesses: Helios and
Aigle.[59] "Aigle" is the "light," also the light of the moon.[60] Although
spiritual, the gift of the Charites remains the *most naturally* spiritual: the
ineffable Charis. That is what was produced by the round-dance of the
changing moon, the celestial prototype of the Charites' dance, as this was
taken up in Greek vision and Greek feeling.

Many are the trinities of sisters in Greek mythology who embody
that primordial round-dance. Among these trinities are placed the three
playmates of the pair of Goddesses, Leto and Niobe. Trinity and Pair seem
to be united here, and yet the group of three belong more closely together.
They are obviously the younger ones. Phoibe is smaller than either Niobe
or Leto. In the foreground kneel Aglaie and Hilaeira. They are lost in
play. Leto, Niobe, and Phoibe stand in the background. From the
picture the situation is clear to read. The five-stone game is being played
In this game five small bones are thrown into the air and intercepted with
the back of the hand. Aglaie and Hilaeira are not the first pair of players
here. From an earlier, interrupted game left-over bones are lying on the
ground. Leto, who is standing there with a black look on her face, has
stepped among them. Niobe, who is being lightly pushed by Phoibe, is
seeking to conciliate the angry one. Clearly it was Leto and Niobe who
had played the game earlier and not finished it. For someone had to lose,
and the one who was going to be the loser in that game did not want to
continue playing and thus offended the one who was winning. It could
only have been Niobe, who in this manner demonstrated the disposition
that always was characteristic of her: always wanting only to win,

77

NIOBE

Philonikia. The younger ones go on playing. One will always be the loser and have to give in. And the winner will play further with the next partner until she too is defeated. But the round will always start over again: a game which, as it appears when seen through the round-dance of the units three and two, is won not only by the victor but also by the loser. Even Niobe would like to step back into the round which she interrupted.

Her tragic mistake was that she allowed the circle to fall apart. She wanted to have only one side of it, the brighter side. And she also stayed caught in *one* side. In this way her mythologem becomes meaningful for us. As Moon-Goddess, for whom the darker aspect predominated, Niobe belonged to Asia Minor where the traces of her cult were maintained and where her name has its linguistic parallels. But the Greeks recognized in her the primordial mother of mankind, an aspect of the feminine in humans: the feminine which bears suffering on earth as the suffering of a mother, not as the travail of birth-giving, but rather as soul-suffering. As seen in the heavens and apart from mankind, the Moon-Goddess became this kind of a bearer of suffering. For easily is the moon's cup filled with the human in our world when this is elevated to a human world like that of the Greeks. Whoever is there fixed in *one* hemisphere, even if it be a God or Goddess, does not enjoy eternal return and, congealed, laments: a primordial image of man's fate, the endless dying of daughters and sons.

NOTES AND REFERENCES

1 Ovid, *Metamorphosis*, VI, 146-316.

2 These documents are published by K. B. Stark in *Niobe und die Niobiden*, Leipzig, 1863. This work, perhaps the most beautiful example of humanistic archeological research, was not properly pursued further. It presents all the material – literary, artistic, and mythological – that was known at that time. The most recent good review of the material is by Lesky in Pauly-Wissowas, *Realencyclopädie*.

3 According to an open lecture, published by E. Mass in *Die Schmerzensmutter der Antike*, Neue Jahrbücher 14, 1911, pp. 23ff.

4 Cf. K. Schefold, "Tochter der Niobe," *Phoebus* 1, 1946, pp. 49ff.

5 Pausanias, V, 11.

6 G. van der Leeuw, "Der Mensch und die Religion," in H. Schmalenbach's *Philosophia Universalis* 2, Basel, 1941, p. 122.

7 The term for the characteristically Christian conception for the "infinite distance between the divine and the human" comes from Rudolf Kassner.

8 Athenagoras, *Legatio pro Christianis*, 14.

9 Vitelli-Norsa, *Papiri greci e latini*, XI, Firenze, 1935, Nr. 1208, in R. Cantarella, *Eschilo* I, Firenze, 1941, pp. 328ff. The crucial lines are in Plato's *Republic*, 380B.

10 Recognized by K. Reinhardt, *Hermes*, 69, 1934, pp. 223ff. He thinks of Leto. Cf. also his *Sophokles*, Frankfurt a. M., 1933, p. 23. Lesky, *op. cit.*, p. 651, thinks of Hermes, though only at the end of the work. Pfeiffer, *Philol.* 89, 1934, pp. 1ff. cites the words of Apollo in Aeschylus' *Eumenides*, 314. For Hermes stepping up to the rancorous Achilles and speaking to him in the *Hektoros Lytra* of Aeschylus, cf. *Vita Aeschyli*, 23-24, ed. Murray.

NOTES AND REFERENCES

11 Printed in Roscher's *Ausführliches Lexikon*, III, pp. 407.

12 The quotations from Homer are in the translation of Richmard Lattimore.

13 Cf. R. Reitzenstein, *Hellenistische Wundererzählungen*, Leipzig, 1906, pp. 84ff.; the author's *Die griechisch-orientalische Romanliteratur*, Tübingen, 1927, pp. 2ff.

14 Artemidorus, *Onirocritica*, IV, 47.

15 E. Samter, "Le Pitture parietali del Colombario di Villa Pamfili," *Römische Mitteilungen*, 8, 1893, p. 142.

16 Stark, pp. 164ff.; O. Jahn, *Abhandlungen Akademica München* 7, 1857, pp. 231ff.

17 Stark, p. 165.

18 Pausanias, V, 11, 6.

19 Cf. S. Eitrem, "De Prometheo," *Eranos* 44, 1946, p. 16.

20 Plato, *Timaeus*, 706B.

21 Eusebius, *Praeparatio Evangelica*, p. 55; Apollodorus, *Bibliotheca*, II, 1.

22 Scholium on Homer's *Iliad*, XXIV, 602; Stark, pp. 354ff.

23 Stark, pp. 361ff.

24 Above, p. 4.

25 Stark, p. 445.

26 Stark, *ibid*.

27 Cf. G. van der Leeuw, *Der Mensch und die Religion*, p. 21; precisely, "world" (Old High German *weralt*, Dutch *wereld*) denotes "age of mankind."

28 Cf. author's *Prometheus: Archetypal Image of Human Existence*, translated by Ralph Manheim, New York and London, 1963.

29 C. Meinhof, *Afrikanische Märchen*, p. 200; author's *Antike Religion*, Bd. VII of the Complete Works, München, 1971, pp. 31ff.

30 Hesiod, *The Work and Days*, 108; author's *Prometheus*, p. 15.

NOTES AND REFERENCES

31 Hesiod, *Theogony*, 521-522. A comparison is the facade painting of the Museo Gregoriano, published in the author's *Prometheus.* The coalescence of Atlas and Prometheus is a parallel to the composition, as conceived above. Behind Atlas a snake indicates the realm of the Hesperides

32 Aeschylus, *Prometheus Bound*, 1025: *kelainobrōton d'epar ekthoinēsetai.*

33 E. Lobel and D. L. Page, *Poetarum Lesbiorum Fragmenta*, fragment 27.

34 *tous d'ara tēi dekatēi thapson theoi Ouraniōnes.*

35 *Iliad*, Book XXIII, 175.

36 *laous de lithous poiēse Kroniōn.*

37 Cf. Lesky, *op. cit.* If the numbers eighteen and nineteen are explained such that the spared daughter or two spared children are not counted, then the fundamental number remains twenty, the correct two-thirds of the month.

38 Cf. W. H. Roscher, 'Die enneadischen und hebdomadischen Fristen und Wochen der ältesten Griechen," *Abhandlungen der sächsischen Gesellschaft der Wissenschaften*, Leipzig, 21, 1903, pp. 4ff. and "Enneadischen Studien," *ibid.*, 26, 1907, 1ff.; on Niobe's children, p. 16.

39 The reference is to the fourteen wooden dolls burned during the Daidala Festival, the fourteen "sacrificed" to Medea in Corinth, the fourteen Athenian boys and girls brought to the Minotaur on Crete.

40 The Homeric Hymn "To Apollo," 91.

41 Cf. M. P. Nilsson, *Geschichte der griechischen Religion*, I, München, 1941, p. 611.

42 Cf. Nilsson, *Die Entstehung und religiöse Bedeutung des griechischen Kalenders*, Lunds Univ. Arsskrift, 1918, 33, 1.

43 Illustrations of her flight in the form of a wolf in Nilsson's *Geschichte der griechischen Religion*, I, p. 506.

44 Cf. C. Robert, *Die Knochelspielerinnen des Alexandros*, XXI, Hallisches Winckelmannsprogramm, Halle a. S., 1897.

45 Pausanias, VI, 24, 6.

46 Ovid, *Fasti*, V, 700; Hyginus, *Fabulae*, 80.

81

47 Presented together in Pausanias, IV, 31, 12.

48 According to the Cypria: Pausanias, III, 16, 1.

49 Pausanias, IV, 3, 2.

50 Pausanias, III, 16, 1; II, 22, 5.

51 Hesychius, s. v.

52 Cf. Eitrem, "Phoibe," in Pauly-Wissowas.

53 Pausanias, III, 14, 6.

54 Pausanias, III, 18, 6; IX, 35, 1.

55 Compare the Roman *Kalendae* which present the same verb with the same meaning.

56 Pausanias, IX, 35, 2.

57 Pausanias, III, 14, 6; XIII, 37, 1.

58 Pindar, *Pythian Odes,* IX, 90.

59 Pausanias, IX, 35, 5.

60 Suidas, s.v.

Afterword

The present book has sprung from the wish to introduce Karl Kerényi's presentation of the *Greek Love Goddess* to the English-speaking reader. The seventh volume in the series of his "Archetypal Images of Greek Religion" (Bollingen Series: Princeton University Press) would have been dedicated to the "Great Goddesses of the Feminine Origin of Life," and among those primarily to Aphrodite, had the death of the author not prevented it. A kernel of this planned monograph, however, is at hand in the chapter "The Golden One" of his *Daughters of the Sun* (Zürich, 1944). It was therefore suggested that this mythological study be left in its context also for the English version, to publish Aphrodite along with the other "daughters of the Sun." Since these images also have a relation to the lunar, it seemed sensible to expand the series with "Niobe."

The first three chapters of *Goddesses of Sun and Moon,* those on Circe, Medea, and Aphrodite, date back to a seminar in the Zürich Psychological Club that Kerényi held between October 15-19, 1943, under the title "Mythological Studies of Greek Goddesses." In the volume *Daughters of the Sun,* they were published as "The Sorceress" (chapter 3), "The Murderess" (chapter 4), and "The Golden One" (chapter 6). The thoughts referring to Hera in the Aphrodite chapter reveal that chapter 5 of the volume *Daughters of the Sun* — "The Partial One" — was devoted to the Queen and Mother of the Gods. She, however, forms the subject of a later work which appeared in 1975 as the fifth volume in the Bollingen Series LXV by K. Kerényi (Princeton University Press) under the title *Zeus and Hera: Archetypal Image of Father, Husband and Wife.* For this reason, the early stage of his presentation of Hera, the one found in the volume *Daughters of the Sun,* was omitted.

Chapter 4 of the present volume, "Niobe," was presented as a lecture at Casa Hutchinson in Solduno (Locarno) during Whitsuntide, 1946, and was first published in the journal *Centaur* (Amsterdam, 1946). After that it appeared as the entitling study in the volume *Niobe* (Zürich, 1949, pp. 13-33).

It is also hoped that this Kerényi text — for whose appearance both the involved publisher and the conscientious translator are to be heartily thanked — will reach the goal expressed by the author in his forward to the collection of studies titled *Niobe* (p. 10): "the making conscious of what once existed as Greek mythology and continues even still to have its correspondence in us human beings. Making conscious is in this case making richer."

Magda Kerényi

Ascona, October 23, 1978